THE
STARFLEET
ACADEMY
ENTRANCE
EXAM

✷ THE ✷
STARFLEET
ACADEMY
ENTRANCE
EXAM

Tantalizing Trivia from
Classic *Star Trek* to *Star Trek: Voyager*

PEGGY ROBIN

A Citadel Press Book
Published by Carol Publishing Group

A Citadel Press Book
Published by Carol Publishing Group
Citadel Press is a registered trademark of Carol Communications, Inc.
Editorial Offices: 600 Madison Avenue, New York, N.Y. 10022
Sales and Distribution Offices: 120 Enterprise Avenue, Secaucus, N.J. 07094
In Canada: Canadian Manda Group, One Atlantic Avenue, Suite 105, Toronto, Ontario M6K 3E7
Queries regarding rights and permissions should be addressed to Carol Publishing Group, 600 Madison Avenue, New York, N.Y. 10022

Carol Publishing Group books are available at special discounts for bulk purchases, sales promotion, fund-raising, or educational purposes. Special editions can be created to specifications. For details, contact: Special Sales Department, Carol Publishing Group, 120 Enterprise Avenue, Secaucus, N.J. 07094

Manufactured in the United States of America
10 9 8 7 6 5 4 3 2 1

Library of Congress Cataloging-in-Publication Data

Robin, Peggy
    The Starfleet Academy entrance exam : tantalizing trivia from classic Star Trek to Star Trek: Voyager / Peggy Robin.
        p.   cm.
    "A Citadel Press book."
    ISBN 0-8065-1695-X (pbk.)
    1. Star Trek television programs—Miscellanea.   2. Star Trek films—Miscellanea.   I. Robin, Peggy.   II. Title.
PN1992.8.S74A34   1995
791.45'72—dc20   95-19253
                                                      CIP

To Karen and Claire, who might, just might,
actually get to explore the galaxy.

CONTENTS

ACKNOWLEDGMENTS

My most gracious thanks to Bill Adler Sr. for creating the idea for this book; Bill Adler Jr. for his helpful writing and for developing so many questions (all those years in front of the TV have paid off!); Paul Baldwin for his most valuable research; Kevin McDonough for his careful editing; Gabriel Caffrey for donating his exceedingly creative *Star Trek* lists; and to our local television stations for broadcasting reruns over and over again.

INTRODUCTION

When the history of television is written a century or so from now, most television shows will be forgotten, remembered only during chance encounters between future starships and television signals that are still traveling through space. But not *Star Trek*, which is destined to become the most famous show of all time. Its fans are probably more numerous and more loyal than are the fans for any other television show. Practically everyone on our planet—and beyond—has heard of *Star Trek*.

But how well do you know *Star Trek*? Sure, we all know that Vulcans have pointy ears, that starships travel faster than the speed of light, that Klingons are bad (or were bad; now they're our friends). But did you know which *L.A. Law* star played a cameo role on *Next Generation*? Did you know who invented the Vulcan nerve pinch? *The Starfleet Academy Entrance Exam* is the book that tests your knowledge about this intergalactic show; it's the book that settles debates; it's the book that's going to entertain you for hours on end, just as the actual television show does.

But not in an ordinary fashion. In *The Starfleet Academy Entrance Exam* you are going to have to test your wits—and spelling counts. This is a test: and if you know your *Trek*, then you'll do okay. If not, just hang your head in shame and walk away. *The Starfleet Academy Entrance Exam* tests all aspects of knowledge about all the *Star Trek* movies and television shows.

PEGGY ROBIN
Washington, DC

HOW TO SCORE THIS TEST

★ You are awarded three points for every correct answer.
★ Subtract one point for each incorrect answer. (Couldn't be simpler!)
★ The bonus chapter at the end of the book is worth 75 points.

Starship Captain (better than being an admiral) 623–700
Admiral   545–622
Commander   467–544
Lieutenant   389–466
Mission specialist on a Starship   311–388
Assigned to a Starbase   233–310
Ensign for life   155–232
Accepted into the academy   78–154
Starfleet reject: Likely to join the Maqui   0–77

1

ALIENS

Q1. In "The Corbomite Maneuver," was Balok, the commander of the *Fesarius*, as menacing as he appeared on the view screen?

Q2. Who gave the orphaned Charlie X his extraordinary and dangerous telekinetic powers?

Q3. What was done to ensure that Charlie X would not endanger any more humans?

Q4. Who has the coldest hands in Starfleet?

Q5. Describe the Ferengi vision of hell.

Q6. How does a Bajoran cleric "read" a person's life-force, which they call a *pagh*?

Q7. How many Orbs have appeared in the Bajoran sky in their history?

Q8. The Bajorans worship the Prophets. Whom do the Ferengi worship?

Q9. Who were "George and Gracie" in *Star Trek IV: The Voyage Home*?

Q10. What does Odo change into in the DS9 episode "The Forsaken"?

    A. A cat
    B. A doughnut
    C. A Klingon
    D. Liquid
    E. Vapor

A1. Not at all. In fact this creature was merely a puppet operated by the real Balok—a friendly alien who was testing the *Enterprise* out of curiosity. The real Balok was the sole crew-member of the *Fesarius*.

A2. The Thasians, a race that had previously been considered to be mythical.

A3. He was returned to Thasus. This was the first example of a story line involving such "returns," which would be repeated several times in future episodes of the entire *Star Trek* saga.

A4. Jadzia Dax. Dr. Bashir noticed it in the third episode of DS9.

A5. Hell is a place of eternal poverty.

A6. By holding their ear very hard (not a pleasant experience).

A7. Nine.

A8. The Profits.

A9. The whales.

A10. D, his natural liquid form.

Q11. In *Deep Space Nine*, what are the Scrian refugees searching for?

Q12. In the *Voyager* episode "Faces," who captured the Talaxian and made him a slave?

Q13. In the first *Star Trek* movie, *Star Trek: The Motion Picture*, we met Navigator Ilia. What effect did she have on humans?

   A. She made them fall asleep if they looked deeply in her eyes.
   B. Human males were very sexually attracted to her.
   C. She made humans smarter by her presence.
   D. She could cure human diseases with a touch.
   E. None of the above.

Q14. In "Family Business" why did Quark have to return home?

Q15. How does Kes help rescue Captain Janeway and Lieutenant Paris in "Time and Again" where they are caught in a time fissure?

Q16. In the episode "Shadow Play," what is special about the aliens who live in an isolated village on a planet in the Gamma Quadrant?

Q17. What is a Serena?

Q18. What is the cause of Jadzia Dax's hallucinations in "Equilibrium"?

   A. Eighty years earlier, Dax had been given an unsuitable host.
   B. The week before Dax drank a bad batch of Quark's liquor.
   C. A year ago she had been subjected to a strong subspace field.
   D. In a previous host she had contracted Rigilian fever.
   E. She is really in love with Dr. Bashir.

A11.　The legendary planet, Kintana.

A12.　The Vedeans.

A13.　B. On her home planet, 114-Delta V, almost everything in life is sexual.

A14.　Because his mother broke Ferengi law that forbids females from earning a profit.

A15.　Kes's growing telepathic powers help locate the two.

A16.　These people are living holograms.

A17.　A Bajoran musical composition.

A18.　A.

Q19. Kes is the only Ocampa on *Voyager.* What is the most unique aspect of her species' physiology?

Q20. Who did Louise Fletcher (of *One Flew Over the Cuckoo's Nest* fame) play in DS9?

Q21. What is strange about the unusually high levels of omicron particles encountered by *Voyager* as it enters a nebula in the episode, "The Cloud"?

Q22. Who wanted Lt. Jadzia Dax's body in the DS9 episode "Invasive Procedure"?

Q23. What gives mission specialist Tam Elbrun, temporarily assigned to the *Enterprise,* special qualifications for communicating with the spaceship-sized creature, and what about him gives Deanna cause for worry?

Q24. Which does not belong with the others?

    A. Rayna
    B. Data
    C. Ruk
    D. Metron
    E. Lal

Q25. Writers of *Star Trek: The Next Generation* have said that Trelane, with virtually unchecked powers, was a prototype for a powerful alien in the later series. Who is that alien?

Q26. What is Kirk astonished to discover about Commodore Mendez?

Q27. In "Devil in the Dark," the pergium miners on the planet Janus VI are being murdered by what they believe is a monster that can eat its way through solid rock, and call on the *Enterprise* for help. Human beings are carbon-based beings; what element forms the basis for this "monster"?

A19. Their life span is only nine years.

A20. Vedek Winn, an orthodox Bajoran religious zealot. The episode was "In the Hands of the Prophet."

A21. The nebula is actually a living organism. When the *Voyager* crew realizes that it has injured this creature, it returns to repair the injury.

A22. A Trill who was rejected as a host, and who longed to fulfill this prestigious role.

A23. He is a full Betazoid and tremendously empathic, however, he is also a former mental patient at a hospital at which Deanna interned, and he's still dangerously unstable.

A24. D. Metron. All the other answers are androids. The Metrons were a highly-advanced, though rather judgmental, life-form, who set up the duel between Captain Kirk and the Gorn captain in "Arena."

A25. "Q"

A26. He is another illusion created by the Talosians to facilitate the return of Captain Pike to their care.

A27. Silicon.

Q28. The monster was called a...

    A. Silicoid
    B. Gonzan
    C. Pergianoid
    D. Horta
    E. Bowli

Q29. Why is the monster, an intelligent and essentially peaceful being, killing the miners?

Q30. In trying to discover the true nature of the creature, Spock uses, for the first time on the series, one of his most formidable gifts. What is it?

Q31. Why did the cloudlike alien in "Metamorphosis" fuse with the dying Nancy Hedford?

Q32. What alien being from *Star Trek* was pictured in a biology exam at a Boston area university?

Q33. In "Lonely Among Us," why are the Antican and Selay delegations traveling to a conference of the Federation Parliament?

Q34. Kirk, Spock, and McCoy are kidnapped on the planet Minara by two aliens in "The Empath." What are the names of the aliens?

Q35. Why are the aliens so interested in the empath's reaction to human pain in "The Empath"?

Q36. In the episode "Let This Be Your Last Battlefield," the famous impressionist Frank Gorshin (who also played the Riddler on the Batman television series) took the role of an alien officer who has been trying to track down the same traitor for 50,000 years. What was the name of this traitor?

    A. Cheron
    B. Lokai
    C. Bele
    D. All three of the above

A28. D.

A29. Because they are unwittingly destroying her unborn children, which look like bowling balls without holes.

A30. The Vulcan mind-meld, which allows him to learn about the intelligence of the Horta, but also causes him to experience her pain, since she has been seriously wounded with phasers.

A31. Because the alien was in love with Zephram Cochrane, who was repulsed by the idea of mating with a nonhumanoid being.

A32. The mammoth amoebae-like creature from "The Immunity Syndrome" was inserted in the exam by a playful professor, and was taken seriously by a number of students unwise enough not to be *Star Trek* fans.

A33. To apply for admission to the Federation.

A34. Lal and Thann.

A35. She is a representative of a race on a planet that is soon to be destroyed because of the natural collapse of its solar system. That system also has another inhabited planet, on which a separate race of aliens has evolved. Lal and Thann are representatives of an advanced alien culture that have the capacity to save the people of one, but not both planets, and are trying to decide which is most deserving. Gem's courageous ministrations to McCoy and Kirk bring about a decision in favor of her people.

A36. The answer is C. Cheron is the name of their planet, and Lokai is the name of the hunted traitor.

Q37. Bele and Lokai are used to explore a regular *Star Trek* theme, that of the destructiveness of prejudice. What is the basis of the hatred that Bele and Lokai bear one another?

Q38. What does Bele call Earth humans?

Q39. Like most episodes, "Whom Gods Destroy" featured a scantily-clad female among the aliens. This one, named Marta, was a bit different from the others in that...

    A. she was a good dancer.
    B. she was a convicted poisoner.
    C. she was green.
    D. All of the above.
    E. None of the above.

Q40. What are the Lights of Zetar?

Q41. How did the crazed Dr. Sevrin commit suicide?

Q42. What does the extra-dimensional life-form first met at Farpoint call his place of origin?

Q43. "The Last Outpost" brings the *Enterprise* into contact with the Ferengi. What is it about the females aboard the *Enterprise* that offends Ferengi sensibilities?

    A. They have only two breasts, unlike Ferengi women who have six.
    B. They have hair, unlike Ferengi women who shave their heads.
    C. They are allowed to eat in the presence of men, unlike Ferengi women who do not eat in public.
    D. They wear clothing, unlike Ferengi women who remain naked.

Q44. What must be done before a full-scale meeting between Data and his brother Lore can take place?

A37. Although both are half black and half white, they are mirror images of one another, one black on the right side, the other on the left.

A38. Monotones.

A39. C.

A40. A collective memory force, all that remains of the inhabitants of the planet Zetar.

A41. By taking a bite of one of Eden's fruit.

A42. The Q continuum.

A43. D.

A44. Lore must be assembled from his component parts found in the abandoned laboratory of Data's apparent creator, Dr. Noonien Soong.

Q45. "11001001" is all you need to see to know which aliens are involved in the episode so titled. They are:

    A. the numerators

    B. the Bynars

    C. the Nomads

    D. the Googols

    E. Zerans

Q46. Why do the Bynars hijack the *Enterprise*?

Q47. The Aldeans abduct the children of *Enterprise* crew members in order to replenish their own sterile race. What was the cause of the sterility?

Q48. At the same time, a Starfleet ensign named Mendon is temporarily assigned to the *Enterprise*. From what planet does he come?

Q49. Who issues dire warnings about the nature of the Borg?

Q50. In "Up the Long Ladder," romantic sparks are struck between Commander Riker and a young woman with an Irish brogue who is a leader of the two hundred surviving colonists on the planet Bringloid V. What is her name?

Q51. In "Manhunt," Deanna Troi's mother Lwaxana is again aboard the *Enterprise* in her capacity as an ambassador. Through her telepathic abilities, what does she discover about two Antedian delegates also on board?

Q52. In "The Survivors," the crew of the *Enterprise* discovers two survivors on the planet Delta Rana IV, an elderly couple named Kevin and Rishon Uxbridge. What turns out to be peculiar about Rishon?

Q53. With what great guilt is the Douwd burdened?

Q54. In "The Vengeance Factor," what did the Acamarian outlaw group call themselves?

Q55. Who is Marouk in "The Vengeance Factor"?

A45. B.

A46. Because their own main computer, on their home planet, is malfunctioning, and they needed a large computer to store information temporarily.

A47. A breakdown of the ozone layer that caused excessive exposure to radiation.

A48. Benzar.

A49. Guinan, whose ancient civilization was destroyed by the Borg.

A50. Brena Odin.

A51. That they are assassins, determined to forestall the planet Antede III's petition to join the Federation.

A52. She is in fact an illusion, created by Kevin, who is himself an alien entity, a Douwd.

A53. He used his enormous power to destroy the entire race of Husnocks, after they wiped out the colony on Delta Rana IV.

A54. "The Gatherers."

A55. The ruler of Acamar III.

Q56. Why did Marouk's personal servant, Yuta, attempt to kill the Gatherer delegate Chorgan of the Lomak clan?

Q57. In "The Hunted," why was Roga Danar imprisoned, and why is his escape of such concern to the authorities on Angosia III?

Q58. When his powers are "restored," with what kind of music does Q celebrate on the *Enterprise* bridge?

Q59. In "The Offspring," Data constructed an android child for himself. Who selected the child's sex and facial characteristics?

    A. A computer.
    B. Data.
    C. Lal (the child, herself).
    D. A committee of the Daystrom Institute.
    E. These matters were left to random chance.

Q60. What name was given to the amnesiac alien saved by the *Enterprise* in "Transfigurations"?

Q61. What is in fact happening to John Doe?

Q62. Who are Jeremiah Rossa and Jono in "Suddenly Human"?

Q63. In "First Contact," a sociological surveillance of the planet Malcor III is instituted even though the planet is still under Prime Directive protection. Why is the covert surveillance deemed important?

Q64. Captain Picard shares a bottle of wine with Malcorian Chancellor Durken. What is the wine called?

Q65. In "The Nth Degree," radiation from an alien space probe has a remarkable effect on Lt. Reginald Barclay, who was such a wimp in "Hollow Pursuits" during the third season. What happens to him?

A56. Because eighty years earlier, the Lomak clan had been responsible for the deaths of most of the members of her own clan, the Tralesta.

A57. He had been a soldier in the Angosian army during a previous war, and along with his fellow prisoners had been given biochemical and psychological treatments to enhance his ability to fight. With the war over, he and other veterans of his kind had been regarded as too dangerous to be allowed to stay at large.

A58. He causes a Mexican Salsa band to appear.

A59. C.

A60. John Doe. He was eluding capture by the authorities on his planet.

A61. He is undergoing a metamorphosis in to an energy-based life-form.

A62. They are the same person, a human youth raised by the Talerian captain, Endar; as his son, called Jono; and the grandson of Starfleet Admiral Connaught Rossa.

A63. Because the Malcorians appear to be on the verge of achieving intersteller flight. When the surveillance is discovered because of an injury to Riker, the planet's leaders convince Picard it is too soon for contact.

A64. Chateau Picard. It is from his family wineries, given to him by his brother in the episode "Family."

A65. His intellectual capacities are increased by two orders of magnitude.

Q66. In "Darmok," we meet the Tamarians. Which of the following 20th-century scientists would be most interested in studying this unique race:

    A. Stephen Hawking
    B. Noam Chomsky
    C. Edward Teller

Q67. What is the name of the Tamarian captain who gives his life in the effort to communicate with Picard?

Q68. What was Klim Dokachin's profession in "Unification, Part 1"?

Q69. What was the special gift of the Ullians in "Violations"?

Q70. Why did the Ullian Jev have to be returned home for rehabilitation?

Q71. In "True Q," Q announces that an *Enterprise* crew member is also a member of the Q Continium. Name the "lucky" crew member.

A66. B. Noam Chomsky is one of the most important linguists in the world. What makes the Tamarians different is that their language, based on metaphors known only to their own culture, is unlike any other language and is virtually untranslatable.

A67. Captain Dathon.

A68. He was the quartermaster of a space junkyard.

A69. They had the capacity to telepathically retrieve the memories of other individuals.

70. He had been intruding into others' memories in a way that became a kind of rape.

A71. Young intern Amanda.

2

★★★★★

ALTERNATIVE UNIVERSES, WORMHOLES, AND TIME WARPS

QI. In what episode did the *Enterprise* first travel through time?

Q2. In "The Naked Time," the plague struck different crewmembers with different symptoms. Match crewmember with plague-induced behavior:

    1. Lieutenant Sulu   A. Weepy desire to tell mother he loved her.

    2. Kevin Riley   B. Longing to stroll on a beach with Yeoman Rand.

    3. Spock   C. Singing "I'll Take You Home Again Kathleen," very off-key.

    4. Captain Kirk   D. Swashbuckling search for Richelieu.

Q3. What caused the *Enterprise* to be hurled backward in time to 1969 in "Tomorrow Is Yesterday"?

Q4. Over what state is the *Enterprise* spotted and classified as a UFO?

A1. "The Naked Time," which aired September 29, 1966, had the *Enterprise* travel backward in time in order to escape the effects of the plague contracted on PSI 2000.

A2. 1.-D, 2.-C, 3.-A, 4.-B.

A3. An encounter with a black hole.

A4. Nebraska.

Q5. When Air Force Captain John Christopher's plane is accidentally destroyed by the *Enterprise*, he has to be beamed aboard to save him. It is discovered that Christopher's as yet unborn son will one day lead an important space exhibition, and in order to avoid changing history, it will be necessary to return Christopher to Earth with his memories of the *Enterprise* erased. Which of the following expeditions will his son head?

    A. The first group of Martian colonists.
    B. The first expedition beyond the solar system.
    C. The first manned Earth-Saturn Probe.

Q6. In "The City on the Edge of Forever" Spock speaks of using the equivalent of "stone knives and bearskins." What is he talking about?

Q7. With his device, Spock learns that Edith Keeler, played by Joan Collins, has two possible futures. What are they?

Q8. What is the distance of 3.26 light years called?

Q9. Footage from what government agency was used very effectively on "Assignment: Earth"?

Q10. In the DS9 episode, "Crossover," while Kira and Bashir were returning from the Gamma Quadrant, their runabout suffered a plasma injector leak. When they exited the wormhole, they found themselves in an alternative universe. Where have we seen that universe before?

    A. In the original series episode, "Mirror, Mirror."
    B. In *Star Trek IV: The Voyage Home.*
    C. In "Assignment: Earth."
    D. Nowhere; it was a unique anomaly.

Q11. How many light years from Starbase 85 (the furthest Federation outpost in the Alpha Quadrant) is the point in the Gamma Quadrant where the wormhole opens?

A5. C.

A6. Constructing a primitive tricorder device out of materials available in the New York City of 1930, where he, Kirk, and McCoy find themselves transported through time.

A7. A brilliant woman who is an advocate of world peace, she will either be killed in a traffic accident or, if she lives, lead a pacifist organization whose existence delays America's entrance into World War II long enough for Germany to triumph, resulting in a world in which the United Federation of Planets and the *Enterprise* never exist.

A8. A parsec, amounting to 19.2 trillion miles.

A9. NASA. A variety of technical tricks were used to put characters at Cape Canaveral, without ever filming there.

A10. A.

A11. Seventy thousand light years.

Q12. In "Eye of the Needle," *Voyager* discovers a micro-worm-hole which may provide a path back to Federation space. There's one problem with the wormhole, however. What's that problem?

Q13. How many light years (approximately, of course) was *Voyager* transported?

    A. 10,000
    B. 35,000
    C. 70,000
    D. 120,000
    E. Beyond any means of measuring.

Q14. Rank, in order from shortest to longest, the amount of time traveled by characters in each of these episodes and movies:

    A. Janeway and Paris in "Time and Again."
    B. Kirk, Spock, and McCoy in "City on the Edge of Forever."
    C. Kirk and crew in "Assignment: Earth."
    D. Kirk and crew in "The Voyage Home."
    E. The crew of the *Enterprise*-C.

Q15. The DS9 episode "Meridian" is similar to what famous 20th-century Broadway musical?

    A. Brigadoon
    B. South Pacific
    C. Fiddler on the Roof
    D. Cats
    E. Evita

Q16. What did Dax learn about proto-universes on Stardate 47603.3?

Q17. Who is the first to see Captain Kirk's "ghost" in "The Tholian Web"?

Q18. How far across space is the *Enterprise* hurled by the Kalandan defensive computer?

    A. 450.4 light years
    B. 990.7 light years
    C. 1,325 light years

A12. The wormhole moves through both space and time—it connects to the past.

A13. C.

A14. A, E, C, D, B.

A15. A. To refresh your memory, the planet Meridian appeared out of nowhere. Meridian repeatedly shifted to a different dimension where they have non-corporeal existence for 60 years—then they returned to their physical state. Jadzia and a Meridian resident fell in love, but Jadzia cannot survive the dimensional shift.

A16. Returning from the Gamma Quadrant, Dax brought back a proto-universe in the episode, "Playing God." The proto-universe nearly destroyed the station.

A17. Lieutenant Uhura. This is one of several indications of a special bond between Kirk and Uhura that might have been further developed if the series had stayed on the air longer.

A18. B. This is nothing in comparison to Q, who dislocates the *Enterprise* by 7,000 light years in *The Next Generation's* "Q Who?"

Q19. What is especially poignant about the funeral of Lieutenant D'Amato in this episode?

Q20. Wesley Crusher's work to return the *Enterprise* to its own galaxy by working with the Traveler. He is rewarded by Captain Picard. How?

Q21. What amazing machine was discovered by the crew of the *Tripoli* on the planet Omicron Theta in the year 2338?

Q22. In "We'll Always Have Paris," what was reported by the freighter *Lalo* and the Ilecom star system that also affected the *Enterprise*?

Q23. In "Where Silence Has Lease," the *Enterprise* finds itself trapped in a region of space with no visible stars. The only other object is a mysterious ship. What does it call itself?

Q24. In "Time Squared," a duplicate of the #5 shuttlecraft of the *Enterprise* is found drifting in space. Is there anyone on board?

Q25. In "Yesterday's *Enterprise*," the crew investigates what may be a Kerr loop of superstring matter. What has this anomaly caused?

Q26. Because of this anomaly, who is surprisingly found to be alive aboard the *Enterprise*?

Q27. Does she stay alive for long?

Q28. In "Remember Me," who returns to aid Wesley Crusher in extricating his mother from a warp field bubble?

Q29. In "Clues," what was supposedly discovered near the Ngame Nebula?

A19. He is buried under varieties of alien rock that had so aroused his interest a little earlier.

A20. Despite his youth, he is appointed "acting ensign."

A21. Data, still dormant, was discovered underground, some time after the science colony was destroyed by what would later be identified as the Crystalline Entity.

A22. A temporal distortion caused by experiments being conducted by Dr. Paul Manheim on the planetoid Vandor IV.

A23. The U.S.S. *Yamato*, but it turns out to be a fabrication.

A24. Yes, a double of Captain Picard, due to a temporal distortion.

A25. A temporal rift.

A26. Tasha Yar.

A27. Longer than you'd expect, considering that she promptly volunteers for a suicide mission aboard a time-shifted Federation ship from 23 years before. Her subsequent imprisonment (occurring between episodes) is used to account for the existence of her stunning look-alike half-Romulan daughter, Sela, who turns up in "Redemption, Part II."

A28. The Traveler, the mysterious native of the planet Tau Alpha.

A29. An unstable wormhole.

Q30. What is the cause of systems damage on the *Enterprise* in the "Disaster" episode?

    A. Anomalies caused by a black hole.

    B. Collision with a quantum filament.

    C. A spaceborn entity.

    D. Sabotage by Lore in collusion with the Crystalline Entity.

Q31. In "Cause and Effect," was the *Enterprise* destroyed in a collision with the missing U.S.S. *Bozeman*?

Q32. What device did Data contrive to prevent the *Enterprise* from entering the causality loop?

Q33. In the fifth-season cliffhanger, "Time's Arrow, Part I," why does the *Enterprise* return to Earth on a priority mission?

Q34. What is the significance of the planet Devidia II in this episode?

Q35. Despite his concern about Data, Picard is reluctant to undertake what he sees as a dangerous mission. What surprising reason does Guinan give him for going?

Q36. In "Time's Arrow, Part II," Picard tries to persuade a suspicious landlady that the crew members are a troupe of actors. What play are they supposed to be performing?

Q37. We meet not only Mark Twain in this episode, but also a bellboy who will eventually become Jack London. Which of the following was not written by London?

    A. *The Iron Heel*

    B. *White Fang*

    C. *The Mysterious Stranger*

Q38. In "Timescape," in which time both stands still and rushes forward at fifty times normal, who is likely to die if temporal reality is restored?

Q39. Who begins to laugh hysterically at the "smile" face evident in the almost suspended explosion of the warp engine?

A30. B.

A31. Yes, but because the two ships were caught in a time loop, the crew of the *Enterprise* experienced the disaster again and again, each time being unaware of what was to come. The time loop was finally circumvented and the disaster averted.

A32. He arranged for a number 3 to appear in thousands of coincidences, so that when the captain was called upon to decide whose advice to follow prior to the next collision, Data would focus on the three buttons of rank on Riker's uniform, conclude that Riker's solution was correct, and this time prevent the collision.

A33. Because in excavations of San Francisco, Data's head has been found under circumstances indicating that it has been there for 500 years.

A34. Its inhabitants apparently threatened Earth at the turn of the 20th century. It is through a temporal vortex on the planet that Data is transported back to San Francisco.

A35. She tells him, "If you don't go on this mission we'll never meet."

A36. Shakespeare's *A Midsummer Night's Dream*.

A37. C.

A38. Beverly Crusher, who is seen taking a lethal phaser hit from a Romulan. It turns out that the Romulan was not in fact firing at her, but at an intruder disguised as a Romulan.

A39. Picard, who is suffering an equivalent of "the bends" in terms of temporal dislocation.

3

BEAMING, HOLODECKS, SHIELDS, AND THE INEXPLICABLE

Q1. What was the maximum range of a tractor beam and of a transporter?

Q2. In the period between *Star Trek* and *The Next Generation*, transporter technology was considerably improved in terms of the range across which it could be implemented. How far was the range increased?

Q3. With whom do Troi and Barclay have a stimulating conversation on the holodeck in "The Nth Degree"?

Q4. In "QPid," why does Worf find himself wearing a jaunty Medieval hat?

Q5. How can one transport through a shield around a ship?

Q6. What is the "miracle" affecting Dr. Zimmerman that occurred in the *Voyager* episode "Heroes and Demons"?

Q7. In the DS9 episode, "Past Tense," what technology does O'Brien desperately try to explain to Kira?
  A. Transporter
  B. Replicator
  C. Warp drive
  D. Photon torpedoes
  E. How to program a 20th-century VCR

A1. 100,000 miles and 16,000 miles respectively.

A2. From 16,000 to 24,000 miles.

A3. Albert Einstein.

A4. He has been cast in the role of Robin Hood's sidekick, Will Scarlet, in one of Q's elaborate tricks.

A5. When the shield frequency is known, one can beam, phaser, torpedo or disrupt through shields. This is what Lursa and B'Etor did in the movie *Generations*.

A6. He appeared outside sickbay for the first time.

A7. A.

Q8. How far can one transport?

    A. 1 kilometer
    B. 100 kilometers
    C. 20,000 kilometers
    D. 40,000 kilometers
    E. 50,000 kilometers

Q9. In "The Next Phase," which two *Enterprise* crew members are believed to have been killed because of a transporter malfunction?

Q10. What do they get to do? (Hint: Tom Sawyer got this chance.)

Q11. What's their funeral like?

Q12. What has caused them to in fact become caught in an interspace pocket, and thus invisible?

Q13. When Montgomery Scott is rescued from being suspended in a transporter beam in "Relics," how long has he been trapped there?

Q14. Is Scotty made aware that Spock and McCoy are still alive?

Q15. In "Rascals," which crew members are turned back into children because of a transporter accident?

Q16. Commander Riker meets his doppleganger in "Second Chances." How long ago was this double created, and how did it happen?

A8. Using *Next Generation* technology, it's 40,000 kilometers. Anything more than that is unsafe.

A9. Geordi La Forge and Ensign Ro Laren.

A10. Attend their own funeral.

A11. Geordi's best friend, Data, reasoning that Geordi would want his friends to be happy, has arranged a party with lively music, balloons, and confetti.

A12. An experimental Romulan cloaking device.

A13. Seventy-five years.

A14. No, that fact was deliberately avoided, sidestepping a situation that could constrict future plots.

A15. Picard, Guinan, and Ensign Ro.

A16. Eight years ago during a transporter malfunction, the second Riker was created, only to be unknowingly left behind on an abandoned planet. Lieutenant Riker's character has developed differently from that of Commander Riker due to the differences of life experiences in the eight years of separation.

4

CAPTAINS

Q1. What irrational fear of Captain Kirk's was revealed in "Arena"?

Q2. In terms of the Prime Directive, how does Captain Kirk rationalize the destruction of Vaal in "The Apple"?

Q3. Why was Captain Picard singing loud drinking songs in Ten Forward in the course of "Allegiance"?

Q4. Why was Captain Kirk able to gain some control over Nomad in "The Changeling"?

Q5. What is Jim Kirk's amusingly fitting punishment for Mudd in "I, Mudd"?

Q6. What was corbomite?

Q7. What great risk did Captain Kirk take in having the *Enterprise* go to the planet Vulcan so Spock could undergo the mating ritual in "Amok Time"?

Q8. The rules of Fizzbin, the card game invented by Kirk, depend upon...

    A. the days of the week and phases of the moon.
    B. the weaponry held by the opposing team.
    C. the species of one's opponents.
    D. the secret markings on the backs of the cards.

Q9. What was the new name Kirk was given during his sojourn among the tribe of the Native American-like people?

Q10. How does Kirk persuade the children the Gorgan is evil?

A1. A prejudice against reptiles.

A2. On the grounds that the computer has distorted its original purpose of protection and led to an unnatural stagnation of the planet's culture.

A3. It wasn't really Picard, but a slightly misprogrammed replica who had taken his place on the *Enterprise* while a race of aliens studied the real Picard and representatives of other species to test the dynamics of authority.

A4. Because Nomad, in its damaged state, confused him with the creator of the probe, Jackson Roykirk, known to Nomad simply as "the Kirk."

A5. He leaves *him* behind, surrounded by duplicates of Stella.

A6. It was a fictional explosive material, used as a bluff by Captain Kirk. When the *Fesarius* threatened to destroy the *Enterprise* for trespassing in uncharted regions, Kirk warned that such an attack would cause the corbomite in the *Enterprise* hull to explode and destroy both ships.

A7. He was disobeying orders from Starfleet Command—a breach that was eventually legalized over by an official request by Vulcan.

A8. A.

A9. Medicine Chief Kirok, an honor earned by saving the life of a drowned boy.

A10. By showing them tapes of their healthy parents and then their graves.

Q11. In "The Battle," we learn about the disaster that befell a ship Picard formerly commanded. What was its name?

Q12. Why did the Ferengi DaiMon Bok want revenge against Picard?

Q13. What is the true mission of Lt. Commander Dexter Remmick aboard the *Enterprise* while it is at the Relva VII Starfleet facility in "Coming of Age."

Q14. What has Picard done wrong to warrant such an investigation?

Q15. In the course of "Conspiracy," Picard joins three other Starfleet captains at a secret meeting at planetoid Dytallix B to discuss infiltration of Starfleet by alien forces. Connect the captains in the left hand column with the correct ship in the right hand column.

    A. Captain Tryla Scott   1. U.S.S. *Thomas Paine*
    B. Captain Rixx   2. Starship *Horatio*
    C. Captain Walker Keel   3. U.S.S. *Renegade*

Q16. What episode in the original *Star Trek* series does "Where Silence Has Lease" most resemble?

Q17. In "Samaritan Snare," Captain Picard and Wesley Crusher make the journey to Starbase 515 together in a shuttlecraft. For what reason is each of them going there?

Q18. In "Who Watches the Watchers," one of the natives in the Bronze Age catches a glimpse of Picard and immediately assumes...

    A. that humans are monsters and must be destroyed.
    B. that humans are hairless and emotionless creatures.
    C. that Picard is insane.
    D. that Picard is God and should be worshipped.

Q19. The final, cliff-hanger episode of the third season of *Star Trek: The Next Generation* might also have been titled "Transfigurations." Why?

A11. The U.S.S. *Stargazer.*

A12. His son had been killed at the Battle of Maxia in combat with the *Stargazer,* and he holds Picard completely responsible.

A13. To investigate Captain Picard for the Inspector General's Office.

A14. Nothing. The investigation is a prelude to his being offered the post of commandant of Starfleet Academy, which he refuses.

A15. A.-3, B.-1, C.-2.

A16. "The Corbomite Maneuver" in which another childlike but powerful alien, Balok, exhibits great curiosity about humans and their ways.

A17. Picard is to have his artificial heart replaced, while Wesley is once again scheduled to take Starfleet Academy entrance examinations.

A18. D.

A19. Captain Picard is abducted by the Borg, who begin to transform him into one of their own kind.

Q20. Although the dreadful defeat at Wolf 359 is believed to have been influenced by information gained from the altered Picard, once he is rescued, the tables are turned. How?

Q21. Both Endar and Admiral Rossa demand custody of the boy Jono in "Suddenly Human," putting Captain Picard in the role of Solomon. How does he decide?

Q22. "I was involved with cowboy diplomacy, as you call it, long before you were born." Who spoke these words and to whom?

Q23. What does Picard discover his rank to be aboard the *Enterprise* after having changed his earlier existence in "Tapestry"?

Q24. As a freshman at Starfleet Academy, Jean-Luc Picard scored a unique accomplishment. What was it?

Q25. What other, rather less important, crew member does Picard pretend to be while dealing with the terrorists?

    A. Yeoman Janice Rand.
    B. Ensign Wesley Crusher.
    C. The ship's barber, Mr. Mot.
    D. Garson, the waiter.

A20. Picard himself provides the answer, breaking free momentarily from his Borg-controlled mind to murmur the word "sleep." Data correctly interprets the message, that all the Borg may be put to sleep by reprogramming Picard's Borg-implants to shut down for a rest-cycle. As all Borg minds are receptors of messages from a central computer, when one sleeps, they all must.

A21. Jono thinks of himself in Talerian terms, and Picard awards him to the custody of the only father he has ever known, Endar.

A22. Spock, defending his unusual mission, to Picard.

A23. Lieutenant, Jr. Grade; he is informed by Worf.

A24. He became the only freshman in history to win the Academy's marathon race. This achievement is revealed by Admiral Hanson in the second part of "Best of Both Worlds."

A25. C.

5

★★★★★
CUSTOMS, LAWS, AND THE PRIME DIRECTIVE

Q1. What is Judge Advocate General Phillipa Louvois called upon to decide in "The Measure of a Man"?

Q2. What is the more common name of General Order #1?

Q3. Was Captain Kirk disobeying the Prime Directive when he succeeded in destroying the computer known as Landru?

Q4. When the *Enterprise* requested permission to acquire materials needed for repairs on the planet Eminiar VII in "A Taste of Armageddon," the reply was a Code 710. What did this mean?

Q5. Which is *not* a Ferengi Rule of Acquisition?
   A. A deal is a deal.
   B. Never place friendship above profit.
   C. A wise man can hear profit in the wind.
   D. It never hurts to suck up to the boss.
   E. A phaser in the hand beats a good lie.

Q6. What does "Gul" indicate among Cardassians?

Q7. When did Worf's uniform change color?

Q8. Which is the correct spelling of the following?
   A. Kobayasi Maru
   B. Kobayashi Maru
   C. Ckobashyi Maru
   D. Kcobayasi Meru
   E. Kobayushi Meru

A1. Whether, as an android, Data is a life-form with full civil rights, and thus the autonomy to refuse a transfer to an experimental program for the development of other androids. If her ruling had gone against Data, he would have been dismantled, and that would have been the end of his character on the series.

A2. The Prime Directive, which Kirk always ignored if he was dealing with a machine gone mad.

A3. No, because he persuaded it to destroy itself.

A4. "Under no circumstances whatsoever approach this planet." The phrase was taken up by many Trekkers and used humorously as in "Under no circumstances whatsoever approach this cake."

A5. E.

A6. Gul is a high-ranking Cardassian officer.

A7. When he became a department head—chief of security.

A8. A.

Q9. In the early episodes of *Voyager* what was wrong with Tuvok's uniform?

Q10. Provide the missing word in this Ferengi Rule of Acquisition: The bigger the smile, the sharper the _____.
A. tooth
B. edge of latinum
C. knife
D. phaser
E. None of the above.

Q11. In a stardate, what does the single digit after the decimal point mean?

Q12. In the episode "Is There in Truth No Beauty?" a medallion inscribed IDIC, worn by Spock, was introduced. What did the inscription stand for?

Q13. Who gets in trouble in "Justice"; what was the offense; and what's the penalty?
A. Deanna Troi; reading suggestive thoughts in a high priest's mind; death by stoning.
B. Lwaxana Troi; refusing a Ferengi captain's proposal of marriage; torture by various devices—or marriage.
C. Wesley Crusher; trampling the flowers; death by lethal injection.
D. Data; taking humorous remarks of others too literally; having to deliver a stand-up comedy routine.

Q14. In "Coming of Age," Wesley Crusher went to Relva VII to take the entrance exam for Starfleet Academy. Did he pass or fail?

Q15. In "Pen Pals," it turns out that a crew member has acted in violation of the Prime Directive by answering a space signal. Who took this step? Why?

Q16. What did Wesley Crusher and *Next Generation* viewers have to look forward to following the "Final Mission" episode?

A9. He had two full and one empty pip for a Lieutenant Commander; however, Tuvok is a lieutenant.

A10. C.

A11. The time of day within a twenty-four hour period, with .5 being noon.

A12. "Infinite Diversity in Infinite Combinations."

A13. C.

A14. He failed—but he was only 15, and did well enough to be invited to try again the following year.

A15. Commander Data, in order to save a young girl, Sarjenka, from a planetary disaster.

A16. Wesley would be off to Starfleet Academy after all, where a slot had suddenly opened up for him.

Q17. In "The First Duty" episode what was the significance of the Kolovoord Starburst?

Q18. In "Starship Mine," what new skills does Data attempt to practice with Commander Hutchinson?

A17. This forbidden stunt flying trick was performed by the Nova Squadron at an Academy range near Saturn, resulting in the destruction of five training spacecraft and the death of one of the five pilots. Wesley Crusher was a member of the squadron, and the one to tell the truth about what happened. Even so his credits for the year were erased, while the squadron leader was expelled.

A18. His new programming for small talk. Or, as he earlier puts it to Picard, "I am attempting to fill a silent moment with nonrelevant conversation."

6
☆☆☆☆☆
ENEMIES

Q1. The Gorn, as everybody knows, is an intelligent, warlike creature. If you were combating a Gorn, but needed to talk about something important, what device would you use?

    A. The universal translator.
    B. The *Enterprise*'s computer.
    C. A Vulcan mind probe.
    D. The Gorn language.
    E. None of the above.

Q2. In the "Conscience of the King," Captain Kirk transports Anton Karidian and his troupe of Shakespearean actors aboard the *Enterprise*. But Kirk was not giving the Karidian Company of Players a lift simply for the amusement of his crew. What was Kirk's particular interest in Anton Karidian?

Q3. How did Picard in his child-form convince the Ferengi guard to bring him to the bridge?

Q4. Who was Boothby?

    A. A Starfleet admiral.
    B. Captain Picard's pet poodle as a child in France.
    C. The gardener at Starfleet Academy.
    D. The ancient Scottish ghost who ravished Beverly Crusher.

A1.   A.

A2.   Kirk is convinced that Karidian is actually Kodos, the ex-governor of Tarsus IV, who initiated a massacre that killed members of Kirk's family twenty years earlier.

A3.   He threw a temper tantrum.

A4.   C.

Q5. While the Karidian troupe is aboard in "Conscience of the King," attempts are made on the life of Kirk and another crew member who had been on Tarsus IV. Which of the following in not a true statement?

    A. Karidian is, as suspected, Kodos.

    B. Kodos is behind the murder attempts aboard the *Enterprise*.

    C. Kirk makes romantic overtures to Karidian's daughter Lenore under false pretenses.

Q6. What is bad about Commander Sisko's old friend Commander Hudson?

    A. Hudson is really a Borg.

    B. Hudson is really a hologram.

    C. Hudson is peddling tribbles.

    D. Hudson is a Maqui.

    E. Hudson has been taken over by a buglike creature.

Q7. In the *Voyager* episode "Cathexis," which member of the *Voyager* crew has been taken over by an alien?

Q8. In "Deja Q," what does Q claim has happened to him?

Q9. Who invented the weapon that destroyed Neelix's home world?

Q10. In the DS9 episode "Duet," who tried to make ammends for the Cardassian rule of terror?

Q11. Who was the only Cardassian left on *Deep Space Nine*?

Q12. Why won't Bajor have relations with Klaestron or Valeria?

Q13. To what *Enterprise* crew member did Q give his own extraordinary powers in "Hide and Q"?

Q14. What is the key to destroying the alien creatures in "Operation—Annihilate!"?

Q15. At the beginning of "Who Mourns for Adonais?" the *Enterprise* is rendered motionless by what?

A5. The false statement is B. It is Lenore, driven mad by her need to protect her father from the consequences of his past, who has become murderous. Kirk, while not unaffected by her beauty, is chiefly interested in prying information out of her. In the end, Karidian/Kodos kills both his daughter and himself.

A6. D.

A7. Tuvok.

A8. That he has been stripped of his powers.

A9. Jetrel.

A10. A Cardassian filing clerk.

A11. Garak, who appeared in "Past Prologue," the second episode of DS9.

A12. Because these worlds helped the Cardassians during their occupation of Bajor.

A13. Commander Riker.

A14. Light intensity, as discovered by Dr. McCoy.

A15. An enormous green hand, in reality an energy field controlled by a humanoid who claims to be the ancient god Apollo.

Q16. Does Apollo claim to be from Earth?

Q17. What action by the "witch" Sylvia gives the episode its title in "Catspaw"?

Q18. Had the alien killer in "Catspaw" ever put in an appearance on Earth?

Q19. In "Ship in a Bottle," what villain from the second season appears again on the holodeck?

Q20. What did the rulers of Triskelion, advanced but bored beings who were little more than disembodied brains, call themselves?

Q21. What self-help organization could have benefited the Triskelion rulers?

    A. Alcoholics Anonymous
    B. Parents Anonymous
    C. Gamblers Anonymous
    D. Scared Straight, Inc.

Q22. The blood-sucking gaseous being in "Obsession" materializes on the *Enterprise* but is so put off by the quality of the blood it tastes that it flees. Whose blood did it sample?

Q23. Why should Mr. Spock be glad he did not encounter the character known as Cirl the Knife, a member of the Krako gang on Sigma Iotia II?

Q24. Although they have transformed themselves into humanoids, the Kelvans of "By Any Other Name" originally had a quite different form. What was it?

Q25. What was their original home?

Q26. What dangerous if beautiful guardian did the extinct Kalandans leave behind them in "That Which Survives"?

Q28. What was the title the insane Garth bestowed upon himself in "Whom Gods Destroy"?

A16. He claims that he and a group of space travelers, of which he is the last survivor, visited the Earth and set themselves up as the gods of the ancient Greeks.

A17. When her cohort Korob tries to aid Kirk, she transforms herself into a giant cat and crushes Korob with her paw.

A18. Yes, as Jack the Ripper.

A19. Moriarty, the nemesis of Sherlock Holmes.

A20. The Providers.

A21. C.

A22. Spock's. Copper-based green blood was not what the creature had in mind for supper.

A23. Cirl had a penchant for slicing off people's ears.

A24. They were tentacled beings.

A25. Andromeda, a three-hundred-year journey away.

A27. The holographic destroyer named Losira.

A28. Master of the Universe.

Q29. In the episode "Skin of Evil," who dies (for the first time at least)?

Q30. Who won the post of security chief left vacant by her death?

Q31. In "The Neutral Zone," it was initially believed that the Federation outposts Delta Zero Five and Tarod IX were destroyed by Romulans. Was this correct?

Q32. What does the noncorporeal intelligence that has created the *Yamato* facsimile call itself?

Q33. In "Elementary, Dear Data," a holodeck mistake creates a sentient life-form that takes the name of a famous fictional villain of the Victorian era. What is that name?

Q34. In "Q Who?," why does Q fling the *Enterprise* 7,000 light years across the galaxy to a previously unexplored region?

Q35. In the unexplored region, first contact is made with a spaceship of what race?

Q36. Name the criminal who had abducted Data while staging his apparent death on the *Pike*.

Q37. What race of aliens is encountered for the first time in "The Wounded"?

Q38. What is the name of the legendary supernatural being whose reappearance has the natives of Ventax II terrified in the episode "Devil's Due?"

    A. Gibreel
    B. Garnesh
    C. Ardra
    D. Lucifer
    E. Beelzebub

Q39. Why won't anyone on the *Enterprise* ever talk about the encounter in "Clues" with the secretive Paxans?

A29. Tasha Yar. She is slimed over by a tar-pool-like creature called the Armus—her resurrection and second death are the subject of further questions later on.

A30. Lieutenant Worf—who was better suited for it, many fans believe, in the first place.

A31. No. It turns out they were destroyed by an unknown force—perhaps, it is later decided, the Borg.

A32. Nagilum.

A33. Moriarty, the great antagonist of Sherlock Holmes.

A34. Because Picard refuses to accept Q's request to become a member of the *Enterprise* crew, and he wants to demonstrate to Picard that he needs Q—there are great dangers in space.

A35. The Borg, an immensely powerful humanoid race that has carried the science of cybernetic implants to the point where the Borg have a collective consciousness and lead a hivelike existence.

A36. Kivas Fajo, whose name was derived from that of production staff member, Lolita Fatjo.

A37. The Cardassians. They come into the picture because of the destruction of a Cardassian science station that Captain Ben Maxwell of the U.S.S. *Phoenix* believes to be a military installation. It is made clear that troubles with the Cardassians have existed for some time, in spite of the existence of a current peace treaty.

A38. C.

A39. Because memories of both crewmembers and ship's computers have been erased. Only Data remembers and he was given a direct order by Picard never to speak of it again.

Q40. In "Silicon Avatar," the surface of the planet Melona IV is devastated by a spaceborne life-form. What is it called?

Q41. Which of the following does the Crystalline Entity most resemble:

A. a giant quart of crystal
B. a humongous snowflake
C. a clear glass saucer
D. trillions of tiny grains of powder

Q42. Dr. Kila Marr is assigned to the *Enterprise* to assist in communicating with the Crystalline Entity. Why is she so intent on destroying it instead?

Q43. What is it about the Lysian ship destroyed by the *Enterprise* in "Conundrum" that deeply troubles Captain Picard?

Q44. With their memories erased and having lost all sense of their previous positions and relationships in the episode "Conundrum," the *Enterprise* crewmembers can only guess at who they are and how they work together. The following statements describe some of the assumptions made at first. Which of those below are true and which are false?

A. Data assumes he is the bartender of Ten Forward.
B. Riker and Ro Laren assume they have been lovers.
C. Riker and Deanna Troi assume they have been lovers.
D. Worf assumes he is the captain.
E. Everyone assumes that Kieran MacDuff is the captain's Number One.

Q45. How long ago have the Ux-Mai terrorists who gain control over the behavior of Data, Troi and O'Brien in "Power Play," been exiled to Mab-Bu VI?

A. 200 years
B. 500 years
C. 700 years

A40. The Crystalline Entity.

A41. B.

A42. Because her son was killed in the course of what is believed to be one of its previous attacks.

A43. Its limited weapons technology, leading him to eventually realize that the Federation orders to destroy the military command headquarters of the Lysian Alliance are fraudulent.

A44. All the statements are true.

A45. B.

Q46. Where do the exiled criminals intend to take the ship and why?

Q47. Where on the *Enterprise* do Troi, Data, and O'Brien blockade themselves?

Q48. In "Imaginary Friend," Clara Sutter, a child on the *Enterprise*, develops a disturbing relationship with a little girl who has appeared aboard the ship. What is the true nature of the visiting child?

Q49. What is the actual designation of the Borg that Geordi La Forge names "Hugh" in "I, Borg"?

Q50. It may be possible to take Hugh, an adolescent Borg, and encode him with instructions that would cause him to destroy the entire Borg race upon returning to the collective Borg System. Why does Picard ultimately decide against this action?

Q51. A parody of *Star Trek* "technobabble" was used by *whom* to confuse *who* when *who* took over the *Enterprise* in a *Star Trek: The Next Generation* episode?

Q52. What was the name of the Cardassian Inquisitor played by David Warner, who tortured Picard?

Q53. How many lights did Gul Madred try to get Picard to say existed, against all objective evidence?

Q54. Did Picard ever tell his Cardassian captor what the captor wanted to know?

Q55. Can you name the episode in which Scotty is suspected of being a serial killer of women?

Q56. In "Face of the Enemy," what did Troi awaken to find herself transformed into?

Q57. In "Frame of Mind," Riker seems to be going insane, both in terms of a breakdown at the conclusion of a theatrical performance on the *Enterprise* and his repeatedly finding himself in an alien insane asylum. What is really happening to him?

A46. To the planet's solar polar region, to bring aboard the other prisoners exiled there.

A47. Ten Forward.

A48. Although she has taken human form, she is actually a previously unknown life-form that is draining energy away from the *Enterprise*.

A49. Third of five.

A50. Because Hugh has developed into an individual while aboard the *Enterprise*, and Picard believes it would be unethical to use him in this way.

A51. By Riker to stall the Ferengi pilot from taking over the helm of the ship.

A52. Gul Madred.

A53. Five, when there were only four.

A54. No, but he confided in Troi afterward that he was about to give in when he was rescued.

A55. "Wolf in the Fold," in which the real killer is revealed to be an ancient alien life-form that can take over other people's bodies (in this case chief city administrator on the planet Argelius II).

A56. A Romulan officer named Major Rakal. She has been kidnapped and physically altered to help smuggle a Romulan peace leader aboard the *Enterprise*.

A57. Aliens have kidnapped him while he is on an away mission and are trying to steal his memories.

Q58. In "Descent," Data feels his first emotions. What are they?

Q59. Who turns out to be controlling the Borg?

Q60. What Borg was instrumental in helping *Enterprise* crewmembers defeat Lore?

A58. First, anger followed by pleasure at killing one of the Borg soldiers.

A59. Lore, Data's evil brother, whom he must ultimately destroy.

A60. Hugh, the adolescent Borg that Captain Picard had previously rescued and restored to the Borg collective (in "I, Borg").

7

★★★★★

ENGINEERING

Q1. In "The Alternative Factor," which of the following best describes the appearance of the dilithium crystals crucial to the plot (and the engines of the *Enterprise*)?

    A. Round and quartzlike
    B. Green, irregular, with an inner fire
    C. Flat and silvery like sheets of mica

Q2. What is special about the *Defiant*, a prototype starship, featured in DS9? .

    A. The food replicators produce much tastier meals.
    B. It has a cloaking device.
    C. It has a new type of weapon, a combined tractor beam/phaser.
    D. The *Defiant* can exceed warp 9 for extended periods.
    E. The *Defiant* is a time traveling ship.

Q3. What are Jeffries tubes, and for whom are they named?

Q4. "Metamorphosis" introduces us to a scientist named Zephram Cochrane who is a living legend. What has he done?

Q5. What was the normal maximum speed of the original *Enterprise*?

Q6. After fusing with the alien probe, Nomad not only became vastly more powerful but developed a new purpose in "The Changeling." What was it?

A1. C. But you might have answered with an A. because that is what they looked like in "Mudd's Women."

A2. B. The cloaking device is Romulan.

A3. Scotty's second home; these crawlspaces on the *Enterprise* give access to control circuits when repairs are necessary, and were named after set designer Walter Mathew Jeffries.

A4. He invented the warp drive a hundred years earlier.

A5. Warp factor six.

A6. To destroy imperfect life-forms—such as the four billion inhabitants of the Malurian System.

Q7. If your starship were suffering a catastrophic failure, and you needed to beam down to a planet, which item would you want most to be repaired:

    A. The Heisenberg compensator.
    B. The science station.
    C. The dilithium crystals.
    D. A tricorder.
    E. All of the above.

Q8. Several *Star Trek* episodes revolved around the need for a fresh supply of dilithium crystals for the warp drive engines. By the time of *The Next Generation*, there are far fewer problems in this regard. Why?

Q9. What are nacelles?

Q10. What is the name of the investigating admiral in "The Drumhead," who sees conspiracies all around her?

Q11. In "Birthright, Part I," what causes Data to have his hallucinatory vision?

A7.   A.

A8.   Dilithium is now used to tune the harmonics of the antimatter reactor, rather than as the principle fuel, and is continuously regenerated in the process.

A9.   The long cylinders at the rear of the *Enterprise* that contain the warp-drive engines. The saucer, which has its own sub-warp power system, can be detached from the nacelles in an emergency.

A10.   Admiral Norah Satie, who can't believe that the explosion in the dilithium chamber of the *Enterprise* is simply an accident due to faulty repair work during the overhaul following "Best of Both Worlds, Part II." She gained her reputation when she discovered the infiltration of Starfleet, dramatized in the first year episode "Conspiracy."

A11.   A power surge.

8

✮✮✮✮✮
GADGETS AND WEAPONS

QI. What is a Feinberger?

Q2. Kirk climbed the Earth mountain El Capitan the old-fashioned way in *Star Trek V: The Final Frontier.* How did Spock climb the mountain?

Q3. Where on the *Enterprise* would you find a K-1 circuit, a K-3 indicator or hear reference made to a K-2 factor?

Q4. "A Piece of the Action" was the only *Star Trek* episode in which any member of the *Enterprise* crew was shown trying to operate a certain kind of machine—which was just as well, considering Kirk's problems with it. What kind of machine is involved?

Q5. Which of the following best describes a Jupiter Eight?
   A. an antiquated shuttlecraft.
   B. an extremely potent drink, comparable to a Harvey Wallbanger
   C. a chrome-encrusted automobile

Q6. What was the designation of the title entity in "The Ultimate Computer"?
   A. Daystrom-B
   B. M-5
   C. PT-109
   D. Nomad
   E. Duncil

Q7. M-5 initially seems capable of running the *Enterprise* without any input from Captain Kirk, but then makes a horrendous mistake. What is it?

A1.   A medical scanner, seldom out of Dr. McCoy's reach.

A2.   With jet boots.

A3.   In sickbay; the references are to monitoring devices.

A4.   An automobile.

A5.   C. The gladitorial televised program on planet 892-IV in "Bread and Circuses" is sponsored by the manufacturer of the Jupiter Eight.

A6.   B. This advanced computer, designed by the great Dr. Richard Daystrom, has been inbued with his own thought patterns.

A7.   In a "war games" practice, M-5 gets carried away and destroys the U.S.S. *Excalibur.*

Q8. What does the message "Condition Green" call upon the recipient to do in "Assignment: Earth"?

Q9. In what episode does Spock lie and Kirk seem to go crazy in a ruse to set up a theft?

Q10. What is the Instrument of Obedience in "For the World Is Hollow and I Have Touched the Sky"?

Q11. What is the difference between a photon torpedo and a disrupter bolt?

Q12. In "All Our Yesterdays," what was the atavachron?

Q13. What are the drinks served by Guinan in Ten Forward made of, and who invented the concoction?

Q14. In "Captain's Holiday," what is the Tox Uthat?

Q15. What does Dr. Soong try to implant in Data without success?

Q16. In "The Game," Riker brings back a device from Risa that when worn around the temples generates animated images of shapes falling into funnels. The entire crew soon seems to enjoy playing the game (with two notable exceptions), but not all is fun and games. What's the matter with the game?

   A. It is highly addictive.
   B. It is part of a Ktaren plot to take over the *Enterprise*.
   C. It brainwashed its users to follow preset instructions programmed into the game by the Ktarens.
   D. All of the above.
   E. None of the above.

Q17. Fortunately, one member of the crew is immune to the game, and a familiar character paying a visit quickly grasps its implications. Who are these two puzzle solvers?

A8. Nothing is a signal that the sender is in some kind of trouble, but that no action is to be taken yet.

A9. "The *Enterprise* Incident," in which the theft of the Romulan cloaking device is successful.

A10. It is a tiny computer that can be inserted in the right temple of humans, and can cause pain or even death.

A11. In conception and effect they are much the same, the former being a Federation weapon, the latter the Klingon equivalent.

A12. A machine used to transport the people of the planet Sarpeidon from the pending explosion of Sarpeidon's sun.

A13. No alcohol is served on the *Enterprise* (Scotty would not have been a happy camper for long). Instead the drinks, which can be endlessly varied in flavor and color, are made from synthehol, invented by the Ferengis. It has the advantage of causing an alcohol-like buzz, but one that can be dissipated at will.

A14. It is a possible key to a weapons system, created in the 27th century but hidden in the past, on the resort planet of Risa.

A15. A new circuit chip that would make it possible for Data to experience human emotions. (In another episode Data's able to modify the chip and give himself emotions.)

A16. D.

A17. Lt. Commander Data and Wesley Crusher, on holiday from Starfleet Academy.

Q18. Match the technological artifacts in the left-hand column to the correct object in the right-hand column:

1. It is 200 million miles across.
2. It weighs over five million metric tons.
3. It can repair itself in space with astonishing speed.
4. Its mission has become to destroy that which is imperfect.
5. It contains bio-filters and pattern buffers as built-in safeguards.

A. The Borg ship in "Q—Who?"
B. The Dyson sphere in "Relics"
C. The *Enterprise*
D. The transporter
E. Nomad

A18. 1.-B., 2.-C., 3.-A., 4.-E., 5.-D.

9
★★★★★
HISTORY

Q1. What's the title of the first *Star Trek* episode and when did it air?

Q2. What assignment was Lieutenant Bailey given at the conclusion of "The Corbomite Maneuver"?

Q3. If John Christopher's son was born in 1967 ("Tomorrow Is Yesterday") and accomplished his history-making mission sometime before age 60, when can we expect this mission to occur?

Q4. In the early episodes of *Star Trek*, the term "Starfleet Command" was not yet in use. What term was employed instead?

Q5. What was the first episode of *Star Trek*'s second season?

Q6. Name the second season's Halloween episode that featured witchery and a haunted castle.

Q7. When had the computer space probe called Nomad, encountered in "The Changeling" originally been launched from Earth?
   - A. 2020
   - B. 2090
   - C. 2130

Q8. An episode aired on February 2, 1968, had clear references to the Vietnam War, which was still raging. What was the episode called?

Q9. According to Pavel Chekov, what was invented by a little old lady from Leningrad?

A1. "The Man Trap," which was aired on September 8, 1966, at 8:30 P.M. It was actually the sixth episode to be filmed.

A2. He was assigned to cultural exchange duty aboard the *Fesarius*.

A3. We ought to be on Saturn no later than 2027. Assuming Christopher is around Kirk's age, 35, Saturn could see humans as early as 2002.

A4. "United Earth Space Probe Agency," pronounced, in abbreviation, "you-spah."

A5. "Amok Time." It aired September 15, 1967.

A6. "Catspaw."

A7. The answer is A. It had been designed to seek out alien life-forms, but after being damaged by a meteor, had fused with an alien probe seeking sterilized soil samples.

A8. "A Private Little War."

A9. Scotch. It was impossible to tell whether Chekov really believed this or was just trying to needle Scotty.

Q10. In "The Omega Glory," there are two separate cultures at war with one another on the planet Omega IV. They are called the Khoms and the Yangs. What parallels are these names intended to invoke?

Q11. What has Starfleet bestowed on Spock that makes his seemingly irrational and illegal behavior in "The Menagerie, Part I," seem particularly shocking?

Q12. How long has the so-called Mr. Flint of "Requiem for Methusela" actually lived?

Q13. Which of the following was NOT one of the famous people who were really Mr. Flint down through the centuries on Earth?

    A. Leonardo Da Vinci
    B. Johannes Brahms
    C. P.D. Bach

Q14. Which of the following was the stardate for "Turnabout Intruder," the final episode of *Star Trek*?

    A. 5818.4
    B. 5928.5
    C. 6120.3

Q15. In "The Big Goodbye," the holodeck situation in which Picard and Data found themselves trapped, wearing fedoras, and in Picard's case, a trenchcoat, was a little too reminiscent of an episode from the original *Star Trek* series. What was that prior episode called?

Q16. What is the significance of the year 2364?

Q17. In "Peak Performance," war games are conducted in anticipation of the approach of the Borg. Who is given temporary command of the older starship, the U.S.S. *Hathaway*?

A10. The communists and the Yankees.

A11. He has been promoted to the rank of full commander.

A12. Six thousand years.

A13. C.

A14. The answer is B. A was the stardate for "The Cloudminders," and C would have taken place in the fourth season.

A15. "A Piece of the Action," also involving gangsters.

A16. In "The Neutral Zone," Data makes reference to that being the current year. It is thus used as a basic point of reference by *Trek* historians to date the unfolding events of the series.

A17. Commander Riker.

Q18. When Picard and the archeologist Vash do find the Tox Uthat in "Captain's Holiday," what do they do with it?

    A. Eat it.

    B. Destroy it.

    C. Give it to the Vorgons.

    D. Take it back to the *Enterprise*.

    E. Send it to the Museum of Archaeology at Starbase 1124.

Q19. Who asked Picard to bring back from Risa a Horga'hn statuette as a souvenir?

Q20. What does the Horga'hn signify?

    A. Religious devotion

    B. Chastity

    C. Sexual desire

    D. Prayer for bountiful crops

    E. Nothing—it's simply a decoration.

Q21. What was the final episode of the third season of *Star Trek: the Next Generation* called?

Q22. What is the significance of Wolf 359 in this episode?

Q23. Which episode of *Deep Space Nine* is described below: The Gamma Quadrant aliens love games. At DS9, they became angry because Quark cheated at Dabo. They forced Quark to play another—dangerous—game in which Sisko, Kira, Dax, and Bashi were literal pawns in a game of survival.

    A. "The Nagus"

    B. "The Storyteller"

    C. "Duet"

    D. "Move Along Home"

    E. "Melora"

A18. B. It was the only way to keep it out of the hands of the Vorgon thieves.

A19. Commander Riker; it is often seen in his quarters in subsequent episodes.

A20. C. Riker requested the Hor'gon as something of a practical joke on Picard, knowing that as Picard carried it around, Risan woman would think he was advertising his desire to mate, and make advances to him—and they did!

A21. "The Best of Both Worlds, Part I."

A22. It was the designated rendezvous point for all available Starfleet vessels to join in a defense against the Borg.

A23. D.

Q24. In the DS9 episode, "If Wishes Were Horses," what's the problem?

    A. Horses are trampling through the space station.

    B. Intergalactic ships appear in the shape of horses.

    C. There is nothing to eat on the station except for horse meat, and nobody will eat horses because they're cute and endangered.

    D. Everybody has a hoarse throat.

    E. People's wishes become reality.

Q25. Leonard Nimoy directed the movie, *Star Trek IV: The Voyage Home*. Who directed *Star Trek IV: The Final Frontier*?

Q26. Match the stardate-birth years with the characters (some characters may have been born in the same year):

Stardate 2222:	William T. Riker
Stardate 2230:	Worf
Stardate 2233:	James T. Kirk
Stardate 2237:	
	Hikaru Sulu
Stardate 2239:	Beverly Howard (Dr. Crusher)
Stardate 2245:	Pavel Chekov
Stardate 2261:	
Stardate 2305:	Jean-Luc Picard
Stardate 2324:	Wesley Crusher
Stardate 2335:	David Marcus, Carol Marcus, Jim Kirk
	Geordi La Forge
Stardate 2338:	Deanna Troi
	Spock
Stardate 2340:	Nyota Uhura
	Ro Laren
Stardate 2349:	Montgomery Scott

Q27. When did James T. Kirk enter Starfleet Academy?

Q28. In "The Squire of Gothos," Trelane's castle was crammed with expensive-looking antiques. But if your eyes were sharp you might have noticed a distinctly odd, but familiar anachronism placed in an alcove near the front door. What was it?

A24. E.

A25. William Shatner.

A26.

Stardate 2222:	Montgomery Scott
Stardate 2230:	Spock
Stardate 2233:	James T. Kirk
Stardate 2237:	Hikaru Sulu
Stardate 2239:	Nyota Uhura
Stardate 2245:	Pavel Chekov
Stardate 2261:	David Marcus, Carol Marcus, Jim Kirk
Stardate 2305:	Jean-Luc Picard
Stardate 2324:	Beverly Howard (Crusher)
Stardate 2335:	William T. Riker
	Geordi La Forge
Stardate 2338:	Deanna Troi
Stardate 2340:	Worf
	Ro Laren
Stardate 2349:	Wesley Crusher

A27. Stardate 2250.

A28. The costume of the Salt Vampire used in "The Man Trap."

Q29. In "The First Duty," for what reason did Captain Picard travel to Starfleet Academy?

Q30. In the attempt to be more human, Data once tried his hand at composing poetry. Which of the following was the name of the poem recited by Data to the less-then-thunderous applause of his audience:

    A. "NCC-1701-D, How I love thee"
    B. "Ode to Spot"
    C. "Press Your Engrams Close to Mine"
    D. "Song of Myself"

Q31. When Riker falls asleep listening to Data's poetry is this just an aesthetic judgment?

Q32. What breed of cat is Spot?

    A. Siamese
    B. Persian
    C. Manx
    D. Somali
    E. Common domestic cat, no special breed

A29. To deliver the commencement address.

A30. B.

A31. No, he is suffering from sleep deprivation because he is being experimented on by aliens.

A32. D and/or E. In his first appearance in "Data's Day," Spot was a Somali breed. In all subsequent appearances, he appears to have shape-shifted, or perhaps been genetically altered into a common house cat.

10

★★★★★

KLINGONS, VULCANS, AND ROMULANS: COSMIC COUSINS

QI. Was the ultra-rational Mr. Spock affected by the disease that released uncontrollable emotions in "The Naked Time"?

Q2. "Balance of Terror" first introduced an alien people who would play a large role in the *Star Trek* sagas down through the years. Were they:
   A. Romulans
   B. Klingons
   C. Ferengi
   D. Trills
   E. Terrans

Q3. At the climax of "Balance of Terror," the enemy ship is destroyed. How?

Q4. What was the name of the episode near the end of the first season in which the Klingons made their debut?

Q5. Why does the Klingon commander Kor look a lot less formidable than the Klingons of Worf's generation?

Q6. What is an S-2 graf unit?

Q7. In "Amok Time," Spock falls prey to a condition called *pon farr*. What is it?

Q8. Who was T'Pring in "Amok Time"?

A1. Yes, his hidden desire for love is exposed, although he still has an instinct to hide when Nurse Chapel reveals her love for him, so that he will not be seen with his defenses down.

A2. A.

A3. The Romulan commander destroys his own ship rather than surrender to Captain Kirk.

A4. "Errand of Mercy," which takes the Klingons and the Federation to the point of war, and is averted by the highly evolved Organians.

A5. Because the Klingon makeup was then quite simple; it evolved enormously over the years.

A6. The Klingon equivalent of the warp drive.

A7. It is the blood fever in the Vulcan mating cycle. If it is ignored, a Vulcan will die.

A8. Spock's bride-to-be, whose demand that the marriage challenge be fought to the death between Spock and Kirk became the central drama of the episode.

Q9. What ordeal (dreadful for him, amusing for the viewer) did Spock undergo in "Friday's Child"?

Q10. In the parallel universe of "Mirror, Mirror," what immediate difference is notable about Spock?

Q11. In "Journey to Babel," we were finally introduced to Spock's parents. What were their names and who played them?

Q12. Why had Spock and his father not spoken to each other in 18 years?

Q13. Connect the Vulcan words in the left-hand column with the correct meaning in the right-hand column.

A. *ahn-woon*	1. First phrase of Vulcan marriage ceremony: "Begin the ritual..."
B. *kah-if-farr*	2. Meaning "all," a fundamental of Vulcan philosophy.
C. *kahs-wan*	3. Most ancient Vulcan weapon, a six-foot band of leather.
D. *nome*	4. Ancient rite of passage, ten days in desert.

Q14. In a moment of stress, Spock for the first and only time refers to Dr. McCoy by his nickname "Bones." In what episode did Spock let down his guard in this way?

Q15. Can you name the episode in which we first see a female Klingon?

Q16. In "The Day of the Dove," Chekov tries to rape Mara, the wife of the Klingon captain, Kang, to revenge the death of his brother at Klingon hands. Did the Klingons actually kill his brother?

Q17. How do Kirk and Kang collaborate to drive out the entity?

Q18. In "Plato's Stepchildren," Spock makes his singing debut. Name that tune.

A9. He found himself forced to hold the new baby.

A10. He has a beard.

A11. They were named Sarek and Amanda, played by Mark Lenard and Jane Wyatt.

A12. Because Spock had opted to join Starfleet instead of embarking on a career at the Vulcan Science Academy.

A13. The answers are A.-3., B.-1., C.-4., D.-2.

A14. "The Tholian Web."

A15. "The Day of the Dove." Her name is Mara.

A16. No—he never had a brother but has been driven berserk by the alien entity that has affected the crews of both the Klingon ship and the *Enterprise*.

A17. By laughing uproariously together.

A18. "Maiden Wine." This was not, of course, a willing performance: Spock is under the control of the telekinetic Platonians.

Q19. "The Way to Eden" featured a band of "space hippies" led by Dr. Sevrin. Which member of the *Enterprise* crew proved to be remarkably sympathetic to the group's antitechnocratic stance?

Q20. What legendary Vulcan peacemaker from the past do we meet in "The Savage Curtain"?

Q21. Which of the following would Mr. Spock refuse to eat (under normal circumstances)?
   A. cheese pizza
   B. filet mignon
   C. asparagus
   D. ice-cream sundae

Q22. Why was it a mistake, in "Heart of Glory," for the *Enterprise* to rescue three crewmen from the freighter *Batris* just before it exploded?

Q23. An *Enterprise* staff physician not previously seen plays a crucial role in "The Schizoid Man." What is this doctor's planet of origin?

Q24. Assuming no authentic Klingon food is available, which Earth dish would a Klingon be most likely to find appetizing?
   A. sawdust-and-mud-pie
   B. metal shavings soufflé
   C. live worms and slugs in a bowl
   D. roast chicken

Q25. In "The Emissary," Worf renews an old romance with Emissary K'Ehleyr. As a result, K'Ehleyr conceives and bears a son, but keeps the child's existence a secret from Worf. What was the child's name, and what was his species?

Q26. What is the Klingon ceremony R'uustai?

Q27. In "The Enemy," what request by Dr. Crusher did Worf refuse?

A19. Mr. Spock, who could be seen in a jam session with the hippies, groovin' on the Vulcan harp.

A20. Surak.

A21. B. Mr. Spock is normally a vegetarian (though in "All Our Yesterdays" he regressed to his ancient ancestors' meat-eating ways).

A22. They turn out to be Klingon renegades who attempt to seize the *Enterprise*, but then don't most aliens at one time or another try to take over the ship?

A23. She is a Vulcan, named Dr. Selar.

A24. C. In "Matter of Honor," Klingons are seen enjoying a worm or sluglike animal—live.

A25. Alexander. He is three-quarters Klingon and one-quarter human, as K'Ehleyr was half-human.

A26. It is a bonding ceremony that Worf uses to adopt Jeremy into his family, although the boy is subsequently sent back to Earth to be raised by an aunt and uncle.

A27. To give blood necessary to saving the life of a Romulan.

Q28. In "The Defector," a Romulan aboard a scout ship being pursued by a Romulan warship asks for asylum on the *Enterprise*. What is this man's rank?

Q29. What warning does Jarok give Picard?

Q30. How does Jarok commit suicide when he discovers that his information was planted by the Romulan government as a test of his loyalty?

Q31. What extraordinary news does the Klingon commander Kurn, aboard the *Enterprise* as part of an ongoing exchange program, reveal to Worf in "Sins of the Fathers"?

    A. That they are brothers.
    B. That he is gay.
    C. That Worf's father is alive.
    D. That Worf will be selected supreme leader of the Klingon Empire.

Q32. What was Worf's father's name?

Q33. In an episode named for him, the second character from the original *Star Trek* (following Admiral McCoy's brief appearance in "Encounter at Farpoint"), made an important visit near the end close of the third *Next Generation* season. Name him.

Q34. He was the original Captain von Trapp in the Broadway production, *The Sound of Music*; she was the original Nancy in *Oliver!* Name these two performers and the couple they played on *The Next Generation*.

Q35. In the movie *Star Trek II: The Wrath of Kahn*, Captain Kirk discovers he is the father of a grown son. What episode of *The Next Generation* uses a similar plot line, and who's the lucky dad?

A28. He initially claims to be a mere clerk, but is eventually discovered to be an admiral, whose name is Alidar Jarok.

A29. That the Romulans are about to establish a base within the neutral zone, an act that is likely to lead to war with the Federation.

A30. He uses poison.

A31. A.

A32. Mogh.

A33. Spock's father, Vulcan Federation Ambassador, Sarek.

A34. Theodore Bikel and Georgia Brown played Worf's adoptive parents, first seen in "Family."

A35. "Reunion" introduces the character of Alexander, who is the son of K'Ehleyr, a Klingon Ambassador murdered by Duras during a time of political turmoil on that planet. The lucky father is Worf.

Q36. When Quark kills a drunken Klingon in "House of Quark," what is his penalty?

    A. The brig.
    B. He must be honest.
    C. He has to marry the Klingon's widow.
    D. He must pay 10 bars of gold latinum to the Klingon's family.
    E. All of the above.

Q37. Who was the Klingon Chancellor in *Star Trek VI: The Undiscovered Country*?

Q38. In the movie, *Star Trek II: The Wrath of Khan*, where was Spock buried?

Q39. What is *Sto-Vo-Kor*?

Q40. Who is the Talaxian scientist who splits B'Elanna Torres into two beings, and why did he do it?

Q41. What level had Spock achieved in computer technology?

    A. A-3
    B. A-7
    C. A-10

Q42. Correctly match the Klingons in the left-hand column with the characterization in the right-hand column, as delineated in the episode "Reunion."

    1. K'mpec   A. Murderous candidate for high council leader.
    2. Gowron   B. Current leader of the high council, who dies of poison.
    3. Duras   C. Installed as new high council leader.

Q43. Geordi La Forge is programmed to carry out a dastardly deed after being kidnapped by the Romulans. What is he expected to do in "The Mind's Eye"?

Q44. What is the significance of the Klingon attack cruiser *Bortas* in "Redemption, Part I," which concluded the fourth season?

A36. C.

A37. Gorkon.

A38. On the Genesis Planet.

A39. The Klingon belief of an afterlife—this is their netherworld.

A40. Sulan. Because of the Phage, a degenerative disease. He needs a "pure" Klingon, so he alters Torres to create a 100 percent genetic Klingon, in the hope that the Klingons' resistance to the Phage will lead him to a cure.

A41. B.

A42. The answers are 1.-B., 2.-C., 3.-A.

A43. Assassinate Kirosian governor, Vagh.

A44. Worf takes the position of weapons officer on the *Bortas* after resigning from Starfleet to avoid conflict of interest because of his special relationship to the new Klingon leader Gowron.

Q45. What is the name of the Klingon family that is trying to undermine Gowron?

Q46. In the fifth-season opener of *Star Trek: The Next Generation*, "Redemption, Part II," a Romulan commander proves to bear a strong resemblance to a former *Enterprise* crewmember. Name the commander and the former crewmember.

Q47. In "Unification, Part I," we meet the third wife of Spock's father, Sarek. What is her name?

Q48. In "Unification, Part II," Picard learns that, far from defecting to the Romulans, Spock is trying to bring about a reunification between the two worlds. But it turns out that Spock himself is being used. To what end?

Q49. Who, to Worf's initial dismay, transfers to the *Enterprise* from the transport vessel *Milan* in "New Ground"?

Q50. What do Klingons consider a pleasant farewell phrase:
   A. "Live long and sweat greatly."
   B. "May you die well."
   C. "Happy trails."
   D. "Hail and farewell."
   E. "Death to traitors."

Q51. What's the connection between Tal Shiar and Tal Shaya?

Q52. Is the commander of the Romulan ship on which Troi finds herself called Toreth or Deceff?

Q53. What legendary Klingon warrior appeared in "Rightful Heir"? Had his character ever appeared on *Star Trek* before?

Q54. Is the Kahless of "Rightful Heir" a legitimate reincarnation?

Q55. To Spock's annoyance, his mother once revealed that he had had the equivalent of a teddy bear as a child. What was the nature of this toy?

A45. The son and other relatives of Duras, traitorous ambition blooming as usual.

A46. The Romulan commander is Sela, who claims to be the daughter of Tasha Yar, who became the consort of a Romulan general when captured in the past in the alternate universe of "Yesterday's *Enterprise*."

A47. Perrin.

A48. As part of a plot by Sela, Tasah Yar's Romulan daughter, Spock is a pawn in a plan to invade Vulcan.

A49. His adoptive mother, Helena Rozhenko, together with his son Alexander, who has been having many problems in adapting to life on Earth. Worf agrees to take custody of Alexander and to raise him on the *Enterprise*.

A50. B.

A51. The Tal Shiar is the name of the Romulan Secret Service, derived from *tal shaya*, the Vulcan term for a swift and painless form of execution, mentioned in "Journey to Babel" in the original *Star Trek*. As the Romulans and Vulcans both sprang from a common ancestor it is not surprising that their languages share many words and word roots.

A52. Toreth. Ensign Deceff beams aboard the *Enterprise* claiming to have a secret message for Picard from Spock.

A53. The warrior Kahless, depicted as a revered prophet in "Flightful Heir," had materialized first in the original *Star Trek* episode "The Savage Curtain," where he was portrayed as one of the great villains of the universe. This is not so surprising, when you recall that he was generated based on the image of him in Captain Kirk's mind, and the Klingons were then much-feared enemies. Kirk's faulty image may also be used as explanation of the fact that Klingon faces appeared much closer to human faces than they appeared to be centuries later.

A54. No, he is a clone of the original, but is accepted even so.

A55. It was in fact a living creature native to Vulcan, a Sehlat with six-inch fangs. Untamed, these creatures could easily rip off a man's arm.

11

LISTS

You really know that you're a *Star Trek* trivia buff when these *Star Trek* lists, created by Gabriel Caffrey, make sense to you. We offer these lists not as questions, but as, well, lists. Take a break from the exam. This isn't a Starfleet trick, so enjoy.

Star Trek Top Ten Lists
© Gabriel Caffrey. Reprinted by permission.

The Top Ten Classes at Starfleet Academy

10. Command 302: Winning in No-Win Situations
9. Communications 101: Opening Hailing Frequencies
8. Space Law 206: Avoiding Court-Martial
7. Navigation 101: Standard Orbits
6. Philosophy 203: Why All Major Systems Fail at the Same Time
5. Command 255: Choosing Minor Landing Party Members Who Will Die
4. Astrophysics 199: Recognizing Unknown Phenomenon
3. Command 309: Creative Obedience to Starfleet Orders
2. Engineering 422: Making Radical Technological Advances Under Time Pressure
1. Space Law 499: The Prime Directive and How to Get Around It

The Top Ten Signs You've Watched Too Much *Star Trek*

10. You send weekly love letters to the actress who played the green-skinned Orion slave girl in episode number 7.
9. You pull the legs off your hamster so you'll have a tribble.

8. You tried to join the Navy just so you could serve aboard the *Enterprise*.
7. Your wife left you because you wanted her to dress like a Klingon and torture you for information.
6. You went to San Francisco to see if you might bump into Kirk and crew while they were in the 20th century looking for a whale.
5. Your college thesis was "A Comparison of the Illustrious Careers of T.J. Hooker and Captain Kirk."
4. You fly into a homicidal rage anytime people say *"Star Trek?* Isn't that the one with Luke Skywalker?"
3. You have no life.
2. You recognize more than four references on this list.
1. You join NASA, hijack a shuttle, and head for the coordinates you calculated for the planet Vulcan.

The Top Ten April Fool's Jokes on the *Enterprise*

10. Everybody act like Riker is the captain.
9. Pretend you've been taken over by an alien being.
8. Program the replicator in Troi's room so that it won't make chocolate.
7. Replay file tape of the Borg ship on main viewer.
6. Tell Data that Starfleet has decided to dismantle him
5. Put a small speaker in Dr. Crusher's bedroom to play garbled voices.
4. Lock Picard in the children's schoolroom with several children and no adults.
3. Substitute some of Dr. Crusher's moss with moss showing 24 hours more growth.
2. Put a sign on Worf's back that says "Kick Me!"
1. Yell into your communicator "Captain, the antimatter containment fields are collapsing."

The Top Ten Ways to Shut Up a Non-Trek Girlfriend (or Boyfriend) Without Killing Her (Him)

10. Tell her "Your ears canna stan the strain!"
9. Vulcan neck pinch.
8. Have an android made of her, then when she starts speaking tell her to "Shut Up!" (See "I, Mudd"—TOS episode.)
7. Wave phaser in her face and tell her you will stun her with it.
6. Use transporter to split her into two separate personalities. Phaser Evil Girlfriend and keep Good Girlfriend. (See "The Enemy Within"—TOS episode.)
5. Tell her you're watching the episode where Picard gets naked.
4. Ask if she wants to see the Picard Maneuver.
3. Try, "Computer—End Program."
2. Tell her she's in violation of the Prime Directive and she is interfering with a lesser developed civilization.
1. Borg her.

Top Ten Reasons Why the Three Stooges Could Easily Take Command of the *Enterprise*

10. Troi would not comprehend their emotions: "Captain, I sense...whoo! whoo!...You numbskull...Why, I oughta..."
9. Riker will be reduced to tears when they call him "Fat Boy."
8. Transporter. Cream pie. You get the picture.
7. Curly could jam turbolifts with his head, rendering security unable to leave their deck.
6. Larry, Moe, and Curly have already been where no man has been before.

5. The *Enterprise* crew will be mesmerized by Curly as he does the Curly Shuffle, and Moe and Larry will take control of the *Enterprise*.
4. Wesley won't be there to save the *Enterprise* in the last few minutes with something he learned in science class.
3. Picard doesn't know the block.
2. If Curly can take a lead pipe to the head, he's just going to laugh at a phaser on "stun."
1. Any stooge can outrun *Enterprise* security.

Top Ten Bumper Stickers for the U.S.S. *Enterprise*

10. "Our other starship separates into 3 pieces!"
9. "One photon torpedo can ruin your whole day...think about it."
8. "HONK if you've slept with Commander Riker!"
7. "Guns don't kill people...Class-2 phasers do!"
6. "Zero to warp 9.7 in 13 seconds!"
5. "CAUTION...We have a trigger-happy Klingon at tactical."
4. "If you can read this...don't you think you're a wee bit too close?"
3. "Have you hugged a Ferengi today?"
2. "We brake for cubes!"
1. "Wesley on board!"
Best bumper sticker on Borg ship:
"Blonde Borgs have the same fun."

The Top Ten Changes if Starfleet Had Sponsors

10. O'Brien would say "Thank you for using the Federation Express transporter. When you absolutely, positively have to get there instantly."
9. Starfleet uniforms would carry Pepsi logos and say "Pepsi, the choice of the *Next Generation*.
8. Main bridge viewscreen would have "VH1" in the corner.

7. Holodeck doors would say "Sony Trinitron System."
6. Communicator pins would be in the shape of an alligator.
5. Mercedes symbol painted on the saucer section.
4. Turbolifts would have "OTIS ELEVATOR" signs.
3. Ten Forward would have a large neon "Miller Litespeed" sign.
2. After communicator beeps, a voice says, "Thank you for using AT&T."
1. *Enterprise* name changed to *American Express Enterprise.*

Surefire Signs That Star Trek Is Taking Over Your Life

1. Saying "make it so" in casual conversation
2. Indignation because the periodic table doesn't include dilithium and tritanium
3. Able to use "variable phase inverter" in a sentence without excessive thought first
4. More than one pair of Spock ears in junk drawer
5. Have figured out the stardate system
6. Sudden urge to wear lots of Lycra
7. Scanning shelves at local liquor store for synthehol
8. The *Star Trek* theme becomes background music for your dreams
9. Major quote sources for thesis are Shakespeare, the Bible, and "The Omega Glory"
10. Memorization of the crew's authorization codes
11. Forgetting that present-day elevators don't have voice interface
12. Attending a convention wearing non-Terran vestments
13. Actual serious thoughts about buying that $300 model of the *Enterprise* from the Franklin Mint
14. Understanding Klingon
15. Lecturing any science professor on how transporters work

16. Playing fizzbin and understanding it
17. "The Outrageous Okona" seems like a fine piece of writing and dramatic stylistics
18. Paying rapt attention during those endless special effects sequences in ST:TMP
19. Inexplicable rock-climbing urges
20. More than three original episode outlines buried in your drawers

Top Twenty Uses for Data's Detached Head

20. Combination paperweight/stapler for Picard's desk
19. The ball in Pariss' Squares
18. Hood ornament for shuttlecraft
17. Replace Troi's broken Chia Pet
16. Scare blind students in braille class
15. Prop open doors for maintenance crews
14. Lawn decoration in arboretum
13. Footstool for captain's chair
12. Entertaining kids in day care puppet show
11. Scare Alexander into doing chores
10. Send to doctor that killed crystalline entity as gag gift
9. Decorative air filter in Picard's fish tank
8. Send to Starfleet Android research center so they can get "ahead" in research
7. Trade to Ferengi for *Star Trek* hologram cards
6. Two words: tether ball
5. Keep Worf's coffee table from shaking
4. Centerpiece in Ten Forward buffet
3. Donate to Starfleet Academy to be head of the class
2. Use as a nutcracker at Christmas time

and the number one use for Data's detached head...

1. Prove to insurance company he died so crew can collect on his life insurance policy

Twenty Things That Never Happen in *Star Trek*

1. The *Enterprise* runs into a mysterious energy field of a type it has encountered several times before.
2. The *Enterprise* goes to visit a remote outpost of scientists, who are all perfectly all right.
3. Some of the crew visit the holodeck and it works properly.
4. The crew of the *Enterprise* discovers a totally new life-form, which later turns out to be a rather well-known old life-form wearing a funny hat.
5. The crew of the *Enterprise* is struck by a mysterious plague, for which the only cure can be found in the well-stocked *Enterprise* sickbay.
6. The captain has to make a difficult decision about a less-advanced people which is made a great deal easier by the Starfleet Prime Directive.
7. The *Enterprise* successfully ferries an alien VIP from one place to another without a serious incident.
8. An enigmatic being composed of pure energy attempts to interface with the *Enterprise*'s computer, only to find out that it has forgotten to bring the right leads.
9. A power surge on the bridge is rapidly and correctly diagnosed as a faulty capacitor by the highly-trained and competent engineering staff.
10. The *Enterprise* is captured by a vastly superior alien intelligence that does not put them on trial.
11. The *Enterprise* is captured by a vastly inferior alien intelligence that they easily pacify by offering it some sweeties.
12. The *Enterprise* visits an Earth-type planet called "Paradise" where everyone is happy all of the time. However, everything is soon revealed to be exactly what it seems.
13. A major Starfleet emergency breaks out near the *Enterprise*, but fortunately some other ships in the area are able to deal with it to everyone's satisfaction.

14. The *Enterprise* is involved in a bizarre time-warp experience which is in some way unconnected with the late 20th century.
15. Kirk (or Riker) falls in love with a woman on a planet he visits, and isn't tragically separated from her at the end of the episode.
16. Counselor Troi states something other than the blindingly obvious.
17. The warp engines start playing up a bit, but seem to sort themselves out after a while without any intervention from boy genius Wesley Crusher.
18. Wesley Crusher gets beaten up by his classmates for being a smarmy git, and consequently has a go at making some friends of his own age for a change.
19. Spock (or Data) is fired from his high-ranking position for not being able to understand the most basic nuances of about one in three sentences that anyone says to him.
20. Most things that are new or in some way unexpected.

12

★★★★★
LOVE AND ROMANCE

QI. Match the lovers:

Man (or alien male)	Woman (or alien female)
1. Christopher Pike	A. Deanna Troi
2. James T. Kirk	B. Vena
3. Spock	C. Zarabeth
4. Worf	D. Anyone who wears a skirt
5. William Riker	E. Minuet

Q2. In "Court Martial" why does prosecutor Areel Shaw bear down so hard on Captain Kirk?

Q3. Was Kirk's defense lawyer named Finney, Cogley, or Stone?

Q4. How did Dr. McCoy save Kirk and Spock from killing one another in "Amok Time"?

Q5. Which was the name given by Eleen in "Friday's Child" to her newborn baby?

    A. Leonard James Akaar
    B. Jamed Tiberius Ma-koi
    C. Miramanee
    D. Bones Scott Teer
    E. Tee

Q6. Which of the Dolman's bodily secretions caused trouble for Captain Kirk? And which of her accessories were useful to him?

    A. Her sweat and her scarf.
    B. Her tears and her necklace.
    C. Her saliva (in her kiss) and her shoes.
    D. Her nasal congestion and her perfume.

AI.   1.–B., 2.–D., 3.–C., 4.–A., 5.–E.

A2.   They had once had a romantic relationship that ended badly (but then, who didn't?).

A3.   Samuel T. Cogley. Ben Finney is the records officer whose supposed death Kirk is being charged with causing, and Commodore Stone is the presiding officer at the court martial.

A4.   By injecting Kirk with a drug that made him appear to be dead.

A5.   A

A6.   B. Her tears acted as a love potion, causing much anguish for Kirk, who had to deliver her to her fiancé on another planet. Her necklace contained dilithium crystals, which enabled the damaged engines to return the ship to warp speed.

Q7. In what episode did Kirk get married?

Q8. Which would have made an appropriate alternative title?
   a. "Kirk marries Pocohantas."
   b. "Who am I, really?"
   c. "Name that tune."
   d. All of the above.

Q9. Why does Deela, Queen of Scalos, seem to have strong amorous designs on Kirk?

Q10. With which *Enterprise* crew member did Lt. Mira Romaine develop a mutual romantic interest in "The Lights of Zetar"?

Q11. Who does, surprisingly, Spock fall in love with in "All Our Yesterdays"?

Q12. On the planet Vulcan and the planet Betazed, childhood betrothals are common practice. In "Amok Time," Spock's betrothed found a way to call off the wedding. In "Haven," we see that Deanna Troi's fiancé is not so keen on marriage, either. Who was he and what happened?

Q13. In "Ménage à Trois," why does the Ferengi DaiMon Tog kidnap Lwaxana Troi?
   A. He wants to ransom her for a fortune.
   B. He wants to trade her for her daughter Deanna.
   C. He has the hots for her.
   D. He plans to sell her to the Pakleds.

Q14. Why is Dai Mon Tog forced to give her back?

Q15. Who accompanies scientist Timicin home for his Resolution ceremony in "Resolution"?

Q16. Why was it rather a mistake for Dr. Crusher to fall in love with Ambassador Olan in "The Host" episode?

Q17. Who volunteered to play host to Odan temporarily so the ambassador could complete his diplomatic mission?

A7. "The Paradise Syndrome."

A8. D, because A) Kirk marries a tribal princess who looks remarkably like illustrations of Earth's Native American heroine, Pocahontas, B) Kirk has lost his memory and forgotten who he is or where he came from, and C) the key to deflating the asteroid turns out to be a combination of notes played in the pyramid.

A9. Because the radiation has also rendered the planet's males sterile.

A10. Mr. Scott, but as usual uncontrollable events stood in the way.

A11. Zarabeth, who is tragically alone in an earlier ice age.

A12. Wyatt Miller had a vision of the woman he was to marry—and it wasn't Deanna. When the *Enterprise* encounters her on the eve of his wedding to Deanna, neither party is insistent on the marriage taking place. He chooses to stay with the woman of his dreams, though she and her race are infected with an incurable virus. Fortunately, however, he's a research doc.

A13. C.

A14. The Ferengi authorities see no profit in offending the Federation over Tog's personal obsession. "There is no profit" in his behavior, and he is disciplined for the breach.

A15. Lwaxana Troi.

A16. Odan is a Trill, one of the parasitic creatures that form a unique bond with its host life-form. Odan is eventually implanted in a female host. (If you answered this question by noting that Gates McFadden, playing Dr. Crusher, was becoming noticeably pregnant, give yourself a bonus.)

A17. Riker; the operation was performed by Dr. Crusher.

Rand, who was in love with Kirk.

nt Riker and Troi, who had been lovers in the past.

Q18. What is Data's particular interest in security officer Jenna D'Sora in the episode "In Theory"?

Q19. Who falls in love with Cirron Connor of the colony on Moab IV in "The Masterpiece Society"?

Q20. From what language is the word "imzadi," what does it mean, and who occasionally uses it in speaking to another *Enterprise* officer?

Q21. In "The Outcast," Riker falls in love with a J'naii named Soren. Why does this present more than the usual romantic problems?

Q22. True or false: Both male and female actors read for the part of Soren.

Q23. Whose wedding aboard the *Enterprise* was scuttled at the last minute in "Cost of Living"?

Q24. In "The Perfect Mate," a gift comes to life too early. What is the gift?

Q25. Who turns into a "sexpot" in "Man of the People"?

Q26. What famous Victorian novel provided the seed for this episode?

Q27. What episode did the writers originally want to call "Murder, My Pet."

Q28. What position has Neela Darren recently taken on the *Enterprise* in "Lessons"?

Q29. What aspect of his life does Picard reveal new things about to Neela.

Q30. Lwaxana is constantly looking for a husband. On DS9, whom does she have her sights set on?

    A. The captain.
    B. The doctor.
    C. The constable.
    D. The restaurant/casino manager.
    E. All of the above.

A18. He wants to establish a romantic relationship to further educate himself about human emotions.

A19. Counselor Troi.

A20. The word is Betazoid for beloved, and Troi once in a while uses it in addressing Commander Riker, with whom she was romantically involved many years before.

A21. The J'naii are an androgynous race forbidden to have inter-gender relationships, which means that Soren will undergo severe "therapy" if she returns to her people.

A22. True. Jonathan Frakes felt that the male/female confusion should have been carried further, with Soren more obviously male.

A23. The wedding of Lwaxana Troi to Minister Campio of the planet Kostolain.

A24. A humanoid female named Kamala. She is a sexual "meta-morph," with the ability to utterly please any partner, and is a gift from the planet Kiros to the chancellor of the planet Valt, to be delivered as part of the reconciliation ceremonies between the two planets. Unfortunately, for the captain, she is released prematurely from her state of stasis and is bound to work her charms on Picard. Since, like Kirk, he's married to his ship, he's able to resist temptation, albeit painfully, and carry out his duties.

A25. Counselor Troi, whose being has been possessed by the ruthless Ambassador Alkar.

A26. Oscar Wilde's *The Picture of Dorian Gray*.

A27. "Aquiel," in which a dog turns out to be a killer alien.

A28. Chief of the Stellar Sciences department.

A29. His experiences from "Inner Light," where he learned to play the flute.

A30. C.

Q31. Who grabbed plasma weap the original s

Q32. A long hinted Chances." Wh

A31. Yeoman

A32. Lieuten

13

★★★★★
MEDICINE, HEALTH, AND BIOENGINEERING

QI. What is the name of the laboratory complex on Gagarin IV in "Unnatural Selection" that is the source of the disease?

Q2. There have been many duplicate Captain Kirks. Match the "Kirk" with what created the duplicate.

1. android duplicate
2. nice, weak Kirk and nasty but strong Kirk
3. power-mad woman hijacking Kirk's body
4. benign ruler temporarily inhabiting Kirk's body in order to construct permanent android body

    A. Sargon's doing
    B. Korby's doing
    C. transporter malfunction
    D. Dr. Lester's life-energy device

Q3. In the *Voyager* episode "Phage," Neelix is saved by the holographic doctor's amazing invention. What is that invention?

Q4. What's the matter with Garak in the DS9 episode, "The Wire"?

Q5. In what episode did the stimulant Cordrazine first make its appearance and who receives an accidental overdose?

Q6. In what episode does Odo first start falling love with Kira?

105

A1. The Darwin Genetic Station, where genetically engineered children possess such powerful immune systems that they have become deadly to other human beings.

A2. 1–B. Roger Korby created the android Kirk in the hope of using it to take over the *Enterprise*.
2.–C. Darn those malfunctioning transporters!
3.–D. Janice Lester could have transported her own mind into anyone's body in the universe, but she chose paunchy old Jim.
4.–A. Sargon was intending to give Kirk's body back, but Henoch *almost* made it a permanent swap.

A3. Holographic lungs.

A4. The Cardassian collapsed and Dr. Bashir had to remove a brain implant in order to save his life.

A5. "City on the Edge of Forever"; Dr. McCoy.

A6. "Abandoned."

Q7. The young girl Miri, in the episode of that name, appears to be about twelve. How old is she in reality? ("Reality"—such as it is.)

Q8. How much longer can she expect to live?

Q9. Why is it that the colonists on Ceti III are not affected by the Berthold rays?

Q10. The spores in "This Side of Paradise" also have the effect of releasing the inhibitions, and causing a sense of peace and love. Which member of the *Enterprise* crew was sufficiently affected by the spores to declare to the beautiful young botanist Leila Kalomi, "I could *love* you"?

Q11. What causes Kirk to become free of the spores?

Q12. In "The Deadly Years," what caused the rapid aging of Kirk and other members of the *Enterprise* crew?

Q13. Why was Dr. McCoy uncharacteristically nervous about performing heart surgery on Spock's father?

Q14. When Kirk was bitten by a deadly Mugatu in "A Private Little War," did McCoy synthesize a serum to save him?

Q15. What is the deepest fear of Lieutenant Uhura?

Q16. Dr. Miranda Jones is the only one who can look upon the Medusan, Kolos, without going mad. What protects her?

Q17. What is Xeno-polycythemia, and who is diagnosed with it in "For the World Is Hollow and I Have Touched the Sky"?

Q18. What episode might have been named "Don't Drink the Water"?

A7. Three hundred years old.

A8. Not much. At puberty, these children will go insane and die, like the adults who embarked on a longevity program three hundred years earlier. McCoy, however, manages to create an antidote (once again).

A9. A plant on the planet gives off symbiotic spores that protect them, even as the plant thrives on the rays.

A10. Mr. Spock. He and Leila, who is among the colonists, met six years earlier and she has been in love with him ever since.

A11. Because anger and other strong emotions cause chemicals to be produced in the brain that deflect the action of the spores. As Kirk watches his crew desert the *Enterprise*, his one real love, he becomes enraged and thus immune. When he discovers the effect of emotions, he deliberately taunts Spock, calling him racial epithets, infuriating him, and provoking him to violence, which releases the Vulcan from the effect as well.

A12. A disease, a form of radiation poisoning spread by a comet. The concept of aging as a disease was right in tune with developing medical ideas in the 1960s.

A13. He had no previous experience performing on a Vulcan.

A14. No, he was healed by the mystical Nona, whose knowledge of healing drugs astonished McCoy.

A15. Becoming old and diseased.

A16. She is blind, but able to disguise the fact from others because her dress is in fact a complex sensor web that allows her to judge distances.

A17. It is a fatal disease with no known cure, and it infects Dr. McCoy.

A18. "Wink of an Eye," since the water on the planet has been poisoned by radiation from the planet's core, causing an enormous acceleration in the metabolism of its inhabitants.

Q19. Match the disease with the patient.

1. Spock   a. Vegan choriomeningitis
2. Kirk   b. Heart valve defect
3. McCoy   c. xenopolycythemia
4. Sarek   d. Rigelian Kassaba fever

Q20. In "The Cloudminders," what was the special value of the rare element called zenite?

Q21. What is the name of the dreadful fever that breaks out on the *Enterprise* in "Requiem for Methusala"?

Q22. What is the antidote for Rigellian fever?

Q23. The crew of the *Tsiolkovsky* is discovered to have been wiped out by a virus similar to the PSI 2000 virus that affected the *Enterprise* crew in what early episode of the original series?

Q24. In "Code of Honor," a plague has killed millions on the planet Stryis IV. What is the disease called?

Q25. In "Symbosis," what was the nature of the cargo saved from the doomed Ornaran freighter *Sanction* and what was it called?

Q26. What was duplicitous about the sale of felicium to the Ornarans by the inhabitants of Brekka?

Q27. In "The Child," Counselor Deanna Troi becomes pregnant without the benefit of sexual intercourse. How did this happen?

A. She was artificially inseminated as part of a biology experiment that went too far.
B. She was impregnated by an unknown alien lifeform.
C. She feigned pregnancy to impress an alien species that reproduces through spores.
D. She adopted a baby by having an orphaned embryo implanted in her womb.

A19. I.–D. Spock feigned illness. Dr. McCoy quick-thinkingly invented Rigelian Kassaba Fever as a ruse to distract the Klevan
guards in the episode, "By Any Other Name."
2.–A. Kirk, as a boy, survived a rare disease, Vegan
choriomeningitis, which left him with the virus in his blood,
which the leaders of Gideon hoped to use to reduce the
population of their crowded planet.
3.–C. McCoy left the *Enterprise* because he was dying of
xenopolycythemia and wanted to spend his last days with
Natira, the high priestess of a planet run by a glitch-ridden
computer. When Kirk and Spock fixed the computer, they
learned it held the cure to McCoy's sickness.
4.–B. Sarek had a heart attack on the "Journey to Babel" but
was saved by open-heart surgery performed by Dr. McCoy
using a blood transfusion from Spock.

A20. It possessed properties needed to fight a plague on the planet
Merak II.

A21. Rigelian fever.

A22. Ryetalyn.

A23. "The Naked Time."

A24. Anchilles fever.

A25. It was a shipment of medicine called felicium, used to control a
200-year-old plague on the planet Ornara.

A26. The medicine was also a narcotic, and the Ornarans no longer
needed it medically, as the Brekka in fact were aware. They
were essentially drug dealers.

A27. B.

Q28. Of the above four choices, which one is not only possible with 20th-century technology, but practiced today?

Q29. What did Troi name her son?

Q30. In "Unnatural Selection," the twenty crew members of the U.S.S. *Lantree* are found dead. What did they die from?

Q31. In whose body is Spock's mind hidden in order to protect him in "Return to Tomorrow"?

Q32. What is Bendii syndrome and what part does it play in "Sarek"?

Q33. After Dr. McCoy develops an antidote in "Miri," what happens next?

    A. Kirk invites all the children to come aboard and travel to Starbase 123.

    B. The children decide they don't want to grow up after all.

    C. Yeoman Rand adopts them.

    D. The Federation sends a sociological team to oversee their development.

    E. Miri and John marry and promise to name their first child Jim.

Q34. In "Night Terrors," thirty-four of the thirty-five crew members of the U.S.S. *Brattain* are found to have died violently. What was the cause?

Q35. In "Identity Crisis," only two out of the following five former crew members of the *Victory*, who contracted a viral parasite on the planet Tarchannan III, survive. Aside from Geordi La Forge, who was the other victim left alive?

    A. Paul Hickman

    B. Emilita Mendez

    C. Susanna Leijten

Q36. What happened to those who succumbed to the virus?

A28. All except B. occurs today—although (c)—feigning pregnancy obviously would not be done to impress aliens, though a woman might try it to trick a reluctant boyfriend into marriage. A., artificial insemination is so low-tech most gynecologists do it as an office procedure. D. is a bit higher tech, though most reproductive specialists can carry it off.

A29. Ian Andrew.

A30. A previously unknown disease that vastly accelerates the aging process.

A31. Nurse Chapel's, an interesting development considering her previously expressed love for him.

A32. A degenerative disease that affects intellectual and emotional stability; it has afflicted Sarek, undermining his abilities until a mind-meld with Captain Picard stabilizes Sarek long enough for him to carry out his diplomatic mission.

A33. D.

A34. Insanity, brought on by dream deprivation, which in turn has apparently been caused by the efforts of an unknown intelligence to communicate with the crew members.

A35. C.

A36. They mutated permanently into nonsentient creatures that are invisible to the human eye.

Q37. Despite the almost miraculous medical technology available to Dr. Crusher and Dr. Pulaski in the 24th century, there is still a malady they can do nothing about. What is it?

Q38. While Chief O'Brien is helping to avert an explosion of the antimatter containment system, his wife Keiko is giving birth. What unlikely crew member assists with the delivery?

  A. Worf
  B. Quinn
  C. Guinan
  D. Wesley Crusher

Q39. What was the baby named, and was it a boy or a girl?

Q40. Why was Dr. Crusher in deep disagreement with neurogeneticist Dr. Toby Russell in "Ethics"?

Q41. In "Tapestry," what does Q tell Picard has happened to both of them?

A37. The common cold. In the episode "Ensign Ro," Picard offers his Aunt Adele's remedy, ginger tea with honey.

A38. A., Worf.

A39. A girl named Molly (who is a regular character as a 2-or 3-year-old child in *Deep Space Nine*).

A40. Dr. Russell wanted to use a highly experimental technique to repair Worf's crushed spine, but she lost this ethical argument in large part because Worf insisted that he would commit ritual suicide if paralyzed.

A41. He claims they are both dead. In actuality, Picard is unconscious and dying in spite of Dr. Crusher's frantic efforts.

14
★★★★★
OTHER WORLDS

QI. In "Shore Leave," a newly discovered planet in the Omicron Delta region, with an Earth-like appearance, seemed to offer an ideal spot for the crew to spend a few days relaxing. Dr. McCoy was the first to discover that all was not what it seemed on the planet. What did he see?

Q2. Which of the following did the planet turn out to be?
   A. A place where fantasies, good and bad, came to life.
   B. An amusement park.
   C. A precursor of the holodeck aboard the *Enterprise* in *Star Trek: The Next Generation.*

Q3. In "The Return of the Archons," what was the eagerly awaited (and dreaded) "Red Hour"?

Q4. What had happened to the crew of the U.S.S. *Archon* when it visited Beta III a hundred years earlier?

Q5. The planets Eminiar and Vendikar have been at war for 500 years, yet there are no outward signs of death or destruction. How could that be?

Q6. In the "Space Seed" episode, the term "the Eugenics War" was introduced to the *Star Trek* vocabulary. What was it?

Q7. The planet Omicron Ceti III in "This Side of Paradise" is regularly bombarded by Berthod rays. What is the danger of these rays?

A1. A human-sized white rabbit pursued by a little girl who appeared to be Alice in Wonderland.

A2. It was all three, designed by an unknown civilization to respond directly to subconscious stimuli.

A3. It was the beginning of a festival on the planet Beta III, during which everyone on the planet was allowed to go berserk.

A4. They had been "absorbed" into the planetary ethos, losing their free will.

A5. The wars were fought by computers on each planet in the abstract. But those designated as casualties dutifully reported to disintegration stations to be destroyed.

A6. The last World War on Earth, supposed to have taken place in the late 1990s.

A7. They disintegrate human tissue, killing a person within seventy-two hours.

Q8. In "The Apple," an ancient, very powerful computer is found to have become the center of the religious beliefs of the inhabitants of Gamma Trianguli VI. What do the natives call the computer?

Q9. The entire planet of Beta III was controlled by a supposedly mystical ruler named Landru. Describe Landru.

Q10. What is quadrotriticale and what is its importance on "The Trouble with Tribbles"?

Q11. In "Bread and Circuses," the *Enterprise* crew assumes that the persecuted people on Planet 892–IV are sun worshipers. Why was this assumption made and in what way was it incorrect?

Q12. On this episode a gladiator in the televised circus events is told, "You bring this station's ratings down, and we'll do a special on you." What were writers Gene L. Coon and Gene Roddenberry up to here?

Q13. What was the monetary unit on Triskelion?
  A. Paraquat
  B. Quatloos
  C. Tri-quads
  D. Quovides

Q14. In "A Piece of the Action," it is revealed that a century earlier, the U.S.S. *Horizon* had visited the planet Sigma Iotia, leaving behind a book, which the planet has made into a kind of societal "bible." What was the book?

Q15. What are the Tribunals of Alpha III?

Q16. What is the inevitable fate of the artificial planet/spaceship *Yonada* is its course is not altered?

Q17. What is the name of the giant computer that runs *Yonada*?

Q18. What was the particular purpose of the planet Elba II?

Q19. Place in history the basis for this planet.

A8. Vaal.

A9. It was a computer, designed thousands of years before.

A10. It is a specialized, highly-concentrated grain. It was the only Earth grain that can grow on Sherman's Planet.

A11. The referred to themselves as the children of the Sun; it is only after returning to the *Enterprise* that Kirk realizes they are actually called the Children of the Son, and that their religion parallels early Christianity.

A12. They were poking fun at NBC and the endless television ratings wars.

A13. B.

A14. *Chicago Mobs of the 1920's.* The entire planet is now run by competing mobs as though it were the Chicago of that period.

A15. Court decisions and/or laws that encompass the major precedents of interstellar law, as put forth in "Court Martial."

A16. It will collide with another populated planet, destroying both worlds.

A17. The Oracle. Kirk finally gains access to it, reprograms it to avoid collision, and from its memory banks retrieves the cure for McCoy's disease.

A18. It was a facility for the criminally insane.

A19. Elba is the name of the island on which Napoleon was imprisoned during 1814–15.

Q20. Why wasn't Eden in "The Way to Eden" the paradise it was believed to be?

Q21. What would you see on a stellar map with the designation 14A?

Q22. What happened on planet Sha Ka Ree?

Q23. How many moons orbit Bajor?
   A. One
   B. Two
   C. Three
   D. Five
   E. No moons—an asteroid passes by every eight days.

Q24. In "The Last Outpost" the *Enterprise* encounters a being who is supposedly from a defunct civilization. That civilization is called:
   A. The Tkon Empire
   B. The Portalli Empire
   C. The Ancient Ones
   D. The Age of Mak-to

Q25. For what reason, in "Justice," was the *Enterprise* planning to make a stop at the planet Rubicon III, and why should they have known better?

Q26. What existed in the narrow electrically conductive zone above the water table of the planet Velara III in "Home Soil"?

Q27. Can you name the mythical planet discovered by the *Enterprise* in "When the Bough Breaks"?

Q28. In "The Outrageous Okona," what are Atlec and Straleb?

Q29. Another nearby colony on the planet called Mariposa is discovered in "Up the Long Ladder." How did five surviving members of the crash populate the planet without incest among their offspring?

A20. Both the soil and the vegetation were poisonous.

A21. Earth's solar system in closeup.

A22. Sha Ka Ree was the mystical planet in the movie *Star Trek V: The Final Frontier*. It is the planet where God was supposed to reside (but didn't).

A23. D.

A24. A.

A25. It was for shore leave; on *Star Trek* shore leave invariably turns out to be a vacation in hell.

A26. An inorganic, intelligent life-form, whose existence was being disrupted by the terraforming team from the federation.

A27. Aldea.

A28. Planets of the Omega Sagitta system that Picard is called upon to mediate between.

A29. They resorted to cloning.

Q30. At the conclusion of "Who Watches the Watchers," Picard is given what that can sometimes be seen in later episodes?

Q31. In "The High Ground," which *Enterprise* crew members are kidnapped by members of a separatist movement on Rutia IV?

Q32. What did the members of the separatist group call themselves?

    A. The Chrysalians
    B. The Ansata
    C. The Koinonians

Q33. Who is accused of murdering Dr. Nel Apgar in "A Matter of perspective"?

Q34. From what planets did two of the other subjects of the study, Kova Tholl, and Esoqq come from? Choose two of the following four:

    A. Cor Caroli V
    B. Mizar II
    C. Gemaris V
    D. Chalna

Q35. What is a class-M planet, like that in "Miri"?

Q36. In "Final Mission," Captain Picard and Wesley Crusher, along with the mining shuttle pilot Dirgo, crash on a moon of which of the following planets?

    A. Gamelan V
    B. Pentarus VII
    C. T'lli Beta

Q37. "Legacy" was the eightieth episode of *The Next Generation*. In the beginning of the episode, the *Enterprise* is en route to the planet Camus II, for the purpose of undertaking an archeological survey of the planet, but instead answers a distress call from the freighter *Arcos*. What is the significance of the mention of Camus II?

A30. A Mintakan tapestry; it is sometimes seen draped over the back of a chair in Picard's quarters.

A31. Initially Dr. Crusher, and subsequently Captain Picard.

A32. B. The Chrysalians were one of the parties trying to gain control of the Barzanian wormhole in "The Price." The Kononians were noncorporeal beings on the planet where Marla Aster was killed in "The Bonding."

A33. Commander Riker is accused of the murder by local authorities, but Riker is exonerated through the use of the holodeck to recreate the circumstances surrounding the explosion that killed Dr. Apgar.

A34. Kova Tholl was from Mizar II (B.) and Esoqq was from Chalna (D.).

A35. It is an Earth-like planet on which humans may walk and breathe without support equipment.

A36. B. Picard is on a special mediation mission while the *Enterprise* under the command of Commander Riker, is dealing with a nuclear waste problem at Gamelan V. T'lli Beta is an initial destination in "The Loss."

A37. The seventy-ninth and final episode of *Star Trek*, "Turnabout Intruder," concerned an archeological expedition to Camus II.

Q38. In "Half a Life," what is the "Resolution" tradition on the planet Kaelon II?

Q39. In "The Inner Light," Captain Picard, rendered comatose by a space probe of unknown origin, lives through a lifetime of memories as another person. What is the name of the long-vanished civilization whose culture and daily life he so vividly experiences?

Q40. In human time, how long does it take the comatose Picard to live out the whole of his Kantaan life from early middle age to old age and grandparenthood?

Q41. What does Picard learn to do while living that other life that carries over into his present existence once he awakens from his coma?

Q42. In "The Chase" what is particularly remarkable about the third dynasty Kerlin sculpture presented to Picard by his former professor, archeologist Richard Galen?

Q43. What secret is contained in the DNA fragments?

A38. Voluntary suicide at age 60.

A39. The Kataan culture.

A40. Under half an hour.

A41. To play a native flute, a talent that will play a central part in a subsequent episode.

A42. When opened, all the miniature figures inside are intact.

A43. They show that nineteen different life-forms on nineteen different worlds, including Cardassians, Romulans, and Klingons, probably evolved from the same basic source.

15

✮✮✮✮✮
PERSONNEL

QI. Who was in command of the *Enterprise* in the episode "Angel One" (featuring Teri Garr)?

Q2. Which two female crew members did Data have a fling with?

Q3. Carolyn Seymour, who played Mirasta Yale, the science minister of Malcor III in the episode, "First Contact," also portrayed another alien. What alien did she play?

Q4. Can you name the young actress and actor who played the title role and the ringleader of the ancient children in "Miri." Both were shortly to appear in Oscar-nominated movies.

Q5. "A Taste of Armageddon" included the character named Robert Fox. Who was he and in what way was he typical?

Q6. The actress who played Assistant Federation Commissioner Nancy Hedford looked immediately familiar to fans of early television. Who was she?

A1. Jordy LaForge.

A2. Ensign Jenna D'Sora and Tasha Yar.

A3. Seymour played a Romulan, Commander Toreth.

A4. Miri was played by Kim Darby, who co-starred opposite John Wayne in his Oscar-winning role in *True Grit* in 1969, while Michael J. Pollard was himself nominated for Best Supporting Actor for 1967's acclaimed *Bonnie and Clyde*.

A5. He was a Federation ambassador sent to establish diplomatic relations with Eminiar VII. He was typical of many Federation envoys in that his incompetence very nearly got the whole *Enterprise* crew killed.

A6. Elinor Donahue, who had played Betty ("Princess") Anderson on *Father Knows Best*.

16

★★★★★
PURE TRIVIA

QI. In the final conversation between Kirk and the Romulan commander, Kirk and his enemy wistfully remark that under different circumstances the two might have become friends. What British poet wrote a poem on this theme (although the enemies in question were English and German soldiers in World War I)?

Q2. Captain Kirk's fantasy in "Shore Leave" caused him to encounter a bully from his past. That meeting also resulted in a series record for the longest something? What record was set in this episode?

Q3. What made the casting of Arnold Moss in "The Conscience of the King" particularly apt?

Q4. With the words "Greetings and felicitations," a troublemaker named Trelane wormed himself into the hearts of Trekkers. Can you name the episode he appeared in?

Q5. In what way was this information about the Eugenics War contradicted by Captain Jean-Luc Picard on *Star Trek: The Next Generation*?

Q6. "The Devil in the Dark" is one of the most beloved and most morally sophisticated of all *Star Trek* episodes. What gave *Star Trek* producer and writer Gene L. Coon the idea for this episode?

Q7. Who directed the most successful *Star Trek* movie of all?

Q8. When did *Star Trek* come to the Soviet Union?

A1. Siegfried Sassoon

A2. Longest fist-fight of the original *Star Trek* series.

A3. Although Moss was the veteran of many television roles, in the 1950s he also headed his own company of actors that toured the country presenting Shakespeare at schools and colleges. He was a natural for the role of Karidian.

A4. "The Squire of Gothos."

A5. He referred to Earth's Third World War as having taken place in the 22nd century.

A6. The idea for the episode came after Janos Prohaska (the makeup and costume genius) crawled into Coon's office wearing a costume he made for *The Outer Limits*

A7. Leonard Nimoy, *Star Trek IV: The Voyage Home.*

A8. On June 26, 1987, when *Star Trek IV: The Voyage Home* was shown in Moscow. The World Wildlife Fund had requested that the film be shown as part of the celebration of worldwide moratorium on whale hunting.

Q9. What role did Colm Meaney (O'Brien) play in the movie
Die Hard II?

    A. Baggage handler
    B. Cop
    C. Pilot
    D. Transporter chief
    E. Villain

Q10. In *Star Trek VI: The Undiscovered Country,* what famous
model played Martia, the shape-shifter who turned into
Kirk?

Q11. Who directed *Star Trek II: The Wrath of Khan*?

Q12. In the original script by Harlan Ellison for "The City on
the Edge of Forever" who prevented McCoy from saving
Edith?

Q13. "Amok Time" was written by one of the giants of science
fiction, Theodore Sturgeon. Which of the following is not
among Sturgeon's many famous works?

    A. *The Dreaming Jewels*
    B. *To Your Scattered Bodies Go*
    C. *More Than Human*

Q14. "The Doomsday Machine," written by Norman Spinrad,
carries deliberate echoes of a great American novel
about an obsessed captain. Can you name the novel?

Q15. What glitch of inconsistency mars "The Apple"?

Q16. Because of budget restrictions many set elements were
reused to represent entirely different locales in separate
episodes. One of the most blatant was the exterior of the
castle in "Catspaw." When had it been seen before?

Q17. Robert Bloch, author of the novel *Psycho*, on which
Hitchcock based his famous movie, wrote three scripts
for *Star Trek*. Can you name them?

Q18. William Campbell (Trelane) has an odd, but decidedly
minor role in American history, outside of his role in
Star Trek. What is it?

A9. C.

A10. Iman.

A11. Nick Meyer, who had directed *The Seven Percent Solution*.

A12. Spock, because Kirk, in love with Edith, is unable to take that step. It was decided that this would undermine Kirk's command authority too greatly, and in the final version it is he who reluctantly sees to it that Edith is killed, as she had been in the reality of his own future.

A13. B. This novel is one of the first of Philip José Farmer's "Riverworld" series, and a Hugo winner.

A14. Herman Melville's *Moby Dick*, whose Captain Ahab is like the U.S.S. *Constellation's* Mathew Decker in his willingness to sacrifice his crew to the pursuit of what he sees as evil personified, in this case not a great white whale, but an out-of-control "planet-killing" machine designed by some unknown alien race.

A15. The pronunciation of the name Vaal varies frequently during the show. Some actors say Vaal as in the first syllable of "volleyball," others as the first syllable in "valley."

A16. As Trelane's grand abode in "The Squire of Gothos."

A17. "What Are Little Girls Made Of," "Catspaw," and "Wolf in the Fold."

A18. He was the husband of Judith Campbell (later, after their divorce, Judith Exner), who had been JFK's mistress—and Frank Sinatra's and Sam Giancana's, as well. The ex-Mrs. Campbell claims that she was the intermediary for requests from the president to organized–crime bosses for assistance in setting up assassination attempts against Castro.

Q19. Who authored the book about the development and filming of the "Trouble with Tribbles" episode?

Q20. What was the special contribution of Fred Philips to "The Deadly Years"?

Q21. Is it true or false that the hairstylist for *Star Trek* was the aptly named Jim Rugg?

Q22. What was unusual about "Elaan of Troilus" writer John Meredyth Lucas?

Q23. "Plato's Stepchildren" featured a television first that put NBC executives into a panic. What was this first?

Q24. One of the writers of "The Lights of Zetar" is better known for her creation of what children's puppets?

Q25. What literary antecedent featured a floating city of upper-class idlers serviced by a land-bound servant class, just as in "The Cloudminders"?

Q26. Which member of the original *Star Trek* crew did not appear as a voice in the animated *Star Trek* series?

Q27. Who plays the green Orion slave girl in "Whom Gods Destroy"?

Q28. The scripts for the episodes "The Child" and "Devil's Due" have a special history. What is it?

Q29. Many of the episodes of the original *Star Trek* series, including the "Errand of Mercy" and the "Omega Glory," are thinly disguised for Gene Rodenberry's view of a contemporary conflict. What is it?

Q30. The very beginning of "The Ensigns of Command" has something missing. What is it?

A19. The book, including the original screenplay, was written by David Gerrold and published by Ballantine in 1973.

A20. This wizard was responsible for the makeup that made William Shatner, James Doohan, and DeForrest Kelley appear 30 years older than their actual ages. Philips added lots of wrinkles, when, as real time has shown, he should have added poundage (at least in two out of three cases).

A21. It is false. Jim Rugg was the special effects chief for all three seasons. Virginia Darcy was the hairstylist for the first season, after which Pat Westmore took over.

A22. He also directed the episode, the only time that the writer and director were the same person during the run of the series.

A23. The first interracial kiss, between Kirk and Uhura, also under the control of the Platonians. Because of the element of duress involved, *Star Trek* executives thought they could get away with it, but NBC made them edit it so that it is impossible to tell if their lips actually met.

A24. Shari Lewis was the creator of Lamb Chop, Charley Horse, and Hush Puppy. Her co-writer on "The Lights of Zetar" was her husband, Jeremy Tarcher.

A25. The "Laputa" episode in Jonathan Swift's *Gulliver's Travels*.

A26. Walter Koenig, Chekov.

A27. Yvonne Craig. She was also Batgirl in the 1960s TV show.

A28. Both were written for a television series that was never brought to fruition, and were then reshaped for use on *The Next Generation*.

A29. The Cold War between the U.S. and Soviet Union.

A30. No stardate is given, a rare omission.

Q31. Is it true or false that Leonard Nimoy came up with the idea for Vulcan nerve pinch?

Q32. What is Planet Hell?

Q33. It comes in three sizes: two feet long, four feet long, and six feet long. What is it?

Q34. Dr. McCoy is said to have had a daughter. What do we know about his daughter?

Q35. The four phrases listed in the left-hand column below are archial codes used by *The Next Generation*'s producers to identify various kinds of story lines. Originally wisecracks, they proved useful in keeping track of scripts and ideas for potential development. Match the code-phrase with the episode that fits properly into the category.

1. Milk Cartons
2. Double Trouble

3. Room with a Q
4. Let's Make Whoopi

A. "Time Squared"
B. "Yesterday's *Enterprise*"
C. "Tapestry"
D. "The Most Toys"

Q36. Of all the guest stars to appear on *The Next Generation* one of the most famous is also regarded as the most dedicated Trekker, a great fan from the start. Can you name this actress who was nominated for Academy Awards in 1948 and 1969, and who appeared in a fourth season episode?

A31. It is true. Nimoy objected to "slugging" Captain Kirk's evil double in "The Enemy Within," feeling it was out of character for Spock to slug anyone. He demonstrated the Vulcan nerve pinch with William Shatner's help, and a unique and very useful aspect of Spock's character was created.

A32. Sound stage 16 at Paramount Studios, as named by the production crew. This is where sets for alien worlds were built.

A33. The *Enterprise* in model form, for exterior shots of the ship in space. The two-foot and six-foot models were made for the start of the series, but directors much prefer the four-foot model that was introduced in the third season.

A34. According to the original character sketches for *Star Trek*, Dr. McCoy's daughter, Joanna McCoy, was a product of a failed marriage; it was this failed marriage that prompted Bones to join Starfleet. Joanna was originally scheduled to make her debut in an episode entitled "Joanna," but the episode was renamed "The Way to Eden." Joanna McCoy did appear in Brad Ferguson's *Star Trek* novel, *Crisis on Centaurus*.

35. 1–D. "Milk Cartons" episodes revolve around missing persons. In "The Most Toys," Data has been kidnapped by a collector of rare objects.
2–A. "Double Trouble" features two of some character. In "Times Squares," a duplicate, though mute, Picard is rescued from a shuttlecraft.
3.–C. "Room with a Q" shows involve that all-powerful alien. In "Tapestry," Q gives a dying Picard a chance to live his life over, differently.
4–B. "Let's Make Whoopi" stories use Whoopi Goldberg in a key role as Guinan. In "Yesterdays," Captain Picard decides to send the *Enterprise* back in time based solely on Guinan's hunch that time has become out of whack.

A36. Jean Simmons, who played Admiral Sattie in " The Drumhead."

Q37. To whom do these contradictory facts, all true, refer: You could hardly see her, and she wasn't there anyway, but it is her voice, and she will be present two episodes later.

Q38. Name the *Enterprise* performer whose varied career has included serving as chorcographer for the Jim Henson productions *Dreamchild* and *Labyrinth*.

Q39. Patrick Stewart directed a "western" episode during the sixth season. Which of the following was its title?
   A. "The Good, the Bad, and the Klingons"
   B. "For a Few Datas More"
   C. "A Fistful of Datas"
   D. "Any Which Way But Here"

Q40. What does Bruce D. Arthur, a mailman in Phoenix, Arizona, have to do with *The Next Generation*?

Q41. What was the name of Troi's western alter ego?

Q42. Patrick Stewart particularly enjoyed working with David Warner, who played the Cardassian Inquisitor Gul Madred, in "Chain of Command." Where had they worked together before?

Q43. What beloved movie classic is recalled in "Birthright, Part II?"

Q44. Who of the following did NOT direct at least one episode of *The Next Generation*?
   A. Jonathon Frakes
   B. Patrick Stewart
   C. Brent Spiner
   D. Gates McFadden
   E. LeVar Burton
   F. Leonard Nimoy

A37. Denise Crosby. During Geordi's brainwashing in "The Mind's Eye," there is a woman in the shadows who is supposed to be the Romulan agent Sela. Another actress stood in for Denise Crosby here, but Crosby post-dubbed her voice, and appeared in the role in the two parts of "Redemption."

A38. Gates McFadden. She can be seen at work as a choreographer in the character of Beverly Crusher teaching Data to dance in "Data's Day." Brent Spiner, in fact, has danced in stage musicals.

A39. C.

A40. He wrote a script on speculation, sent it in, and was given joint credit with Joe Meonsky for the final result, the episode "Clues."

A41. Durango.

A42. They were both members of Britain's Royal Shakespeare Company.

A43. *Casablanca*, when the Klingon warrior chant is used to drown out the Romulans. But you would also be correct if you thought back to an earlier French masterpiece, *Grand Illusion*, which was the first to make use of the warring groups of singers.

A44. The answer is C; he had no interest in doing so.

17

★★★★★
QUOTATIONS

Q1. In "The Man Trap," who uttered the immortal words, "May the Great Bird of the Galaxy bless your planet"?

Q2. Dr. McCoy's much-repeated line, "He's dead, Jim," first showed up on "The Enemy Within." Whose death was involved?

Q3. Fill in the blank in the quotation from Q in the first encounter between the *Enterprise* and that being:

"Thou art notified that thy kind has infiltrated the _____ too far already."

Q4. In which episode does Captain Picard say "Merde"?

Q5. What were Dr. McCoy's immortal words when Kirk asked him to heal the Horta?

Q6. Captain Jellico was not at all happy about an aspect of his ready room in "Chain of Command." Which of the following was the order he gave to Riker to correct the situation?
A. "Get that damned fish out of my ready room."
B. "I need curtains on this window—pronto."
C. "Chairs, dammit! We need some comfortable chairs!"
D. "Get that old name plate off the door. I want to see Jellico up there in capital letters—and I mean today!"

Q7. Who said, "According to myth the Earth was created in six days, now watch out, here comes Genesis, we'll do it for you in six minutes"?

A1. Lieutenant Sulu. Great Bird of the Galaxy was associate producer Bob Justman's joking nickname for series creator Gene Roddenberry.

A2. That of the doglike "space spaniel," who had been divided into two beings.

A3. galaxy

A4. "The Last Outpost."

A5. "I'm a doctor, not a bricklayer." Nevertheless, he fashioned a concrete bandage for its wounds and saves its life.

A6. A.

A7. McCoy in the second *Star Trek* movie. Genesis made life out of inert matter.

Q8. Provide the names of the character speaking the lines identified as A and B.

    A: Do you have orders for me, sir?

    B: Release the *Stargazer* from the tractor beam, Number One.

    A: Sir?

    B: The tractor beam.

    A: Sir, are you abandoning her?

    B: No, but her inertia will carry her along with us, or did you sleep through the Academy lecture on the conservation of tractor beam power?

Q9. Who said: "There are always possibilities"?

Q10. Who said, "A Bajoran draws courage from his spiritual life. Our life force, or *pagh*, is replenished by the Prophets."

A8. **A** = Riker; **B** = Picard

A9. Kirk, when saying goodbye to Spock in the *Star Trek II: The Wrath of Kahn* movie.

A10. Kai Opaka, the head of the Bajoran church.

18

SPACE SHIPS AND OTHER VESSELS

QI. Match ships and passengers:

1. U.S.S. *Antares*
2. U.S.S. *Intrepid*
3. S.S. *Botany Bay*

4. Shuttlecraft *Galileo*

A. An all-Vulcan crew.
B. Charlie Evans
C. Mr. Spock (in command) plus six other quarrelsome crewmembers
D. A slumbering Khan Noonien Singh and his followers

Q2. How many decks did the original *Enterprise* have at the thickest point of its saucer?

Q3. What are a DY-500 and a DY-100?

Q4. Which of the following was the name of the recreation room on the original *Enterprise*?

    A. G-Forward
    B. Area 39
    C. Holodeck One
    D. Liberty Eleven

Q5. What kind of person would be housed on Deck Two of the *Enterprise*?

A1. 1.–B., 2.–A., 3–D., 4–C.

A2. Eleven.

A3. Very early Earth-built interplanetary ships. The *Botany Bay* of "Space Seed" is one of the latter class.

A4. B.

A5. Anyone Captain Kirk wanted to keep under conditions of high security, for the safety of the ship or even of the person involved.

Q6. What is the name of the vanished starship in "The Tholian Web"?

    A. *John Paul Jones*
    B. *Defiant*
    C. *Captain Nemo*
    D. *Farragut*
    E. *Intrepid*

Q7. When Captain Kirk beams down to the planet Gideon in "The Mark of Gideon," where does he find himself?

Q8. What kind of ship is the *Tsiolkovsky*, with which the *Enterprise* has a rendezvous in "The Naked Now"?

Q9. What does Sisko try to build in the DS9 episode "Explorers"?

    A. A model *Enterprise*-A.
    B. A working *Apollo* spacecraft.
    C. A Klingon Bird-of-Prey.
    D. A Bajoran space vessel.
    E. A mini-space station.

Q10. What was the name of the sailing vessel in *Star Trek: Generations*?

Q11. Why did he try to build that Bajoran space vessel?

Q12. What are the runabouts on *Deep Space Nine* called?

Q13. On a Federation starship, what does the prefix NX stand for?

Q14. In "The Arsenal of Freedom," the *Enterprise* is called upon to investigate the disappearance of the U.S.S. *Drake*? What special relationship to this vessel is commander Riker revealed to have?

Q15. What was the very apt, inside-joke name of the derelict spacecraft, first launched at the end of the 20th century, containing the cryogenically preserved remains of a number of human beings, that was encountered by the *Enterprise* in the first season's final episode "The Neutral Zone"?

A6. B.

A7. On what seems to be the *Enterprise* but which is actually a precise replica, minus its crew.

A8. It is a science vessel that had been monitoring the collapse of a red giant star.

A9. D

A10. The *Enterprise.*

A11. To prove that Bajorans could have once visited Cardassia in a solar-wind powered craft.

A12. *Danube*-class ships.

A13. It means that that ship is a prototype; when the ship is fully in use, it receives the NCC designation.

A14. He was offered its command, but declined.

A15. In tiny letters was inscribed S.S. *Birdseye.*

Q16. In "A Matter of Honor," what is the *pagh*?

Q17. For whom is the shuttlecraft in "The Ensigns of Command," which Data uses to travel to Tau Cygna V, named?

Q18. The shuttlepod that apparently killed Data when it exploded in "The Most Toys," was named for an important figure in the original *Star Trek*. What was the shuttlepod called?

Q19. The starship that was supposed to give Wesley Crusher transport to Starfleet Academy was named for a science fiction legend. Name the ship.

Q20. Of what significance to Riker is the starship *Melbourne*?

Q21. In the fourth season opener, "The Best of Both Worlds, Part II," how many Federation and Klingon starships were lost during the battle with the Borg at Wolf 359?
   A. 19
   B. 39
   C. 43

Q22. What is the significance of the number 1,014?

Q23. In "Redemption, Part II" the armada gathered under Picard's overall command included twenty-three ships. Which of the following ships were Riker and Data, respectively, given temporary command of?
   A. *Endeavor*
   B. *Hornet*
   C. *Excalibur*
   D. *Akagi*
   E. *Sutherland*
   F. *Tian An Men*

A16. A Klingon vessel on which Riker temporarily serves as part of an exchange program.

A17. It is called the *Onizuka*, in honor of *Challenger* astronaut Ellison Onizuka.

A18. The *Pike*, after the one-time captain of the *Enterprise*.

A19. The U.S.S. *Bradbury*, after Ray Bradbury, author of *The Martian Chronicles* and other classic science-fiction.

A20. He was offered its captaincy but decided to remain with the *Enterprise*.

A21. B. This is later revealed in "The Drumhead."

A22. It is the number of people aboard the *Enterprise*, as stated by Picard in "Remember Me." This is the episode in which Dr. Crusher becomes trapped in a warp bubble; and the people around her keep disappearing.

A23. C and E.

Q24. In the list of ships in the questions above there are two that were named after opposing vessels at the Battle of Midway in World War II. Can you pick them out?

Q25. One of the most difficult effects created for *The Next Generation* was the re-creation of the bridge of the original *Star Trek* for "Relics." A small section of the original bridge was rebuilt and combined with blue screen footage of the empty bridge from a *Star Trek* episode. Which episode provided a shot of the empty bridge?

A24. The *Hornet* and the *Akagi*.

A25. It was a clip from "This Side of Paradise," in which the crew, infected by spores, deserted the ship.

19

★★★★★
STRANGE CREATURES

Q1. Why is the title character of the "The Man Trap" often referred to *Star Trek* fans as "The Salt Vampire"?

Q2. Which of the following was the name of the large, green reptilian creature with glaring red eyes Kirk had to battle in "Arena"?

    A. Gorn
    B. Goren
    C. Gorgon
    D. Godzigore
    E. Gorndot

Q3. To what does Dr. McCoy ascribe the remarkable reproduction rate of the tribbles?

Q4. Why does it turn out to be a good thing that the rapidly reproducing tribbles start devouring the stored grain in "The Trouble with Tribbles?"

Q5. Why is Kolos, the Medusan ambassador to the Federation, encased in a protective box in "Is There in Truth No Beauty?"

A1. The last surviving native of the Planet M-113, it was a shape-changing humanoid that survived on sodium chloride. It killed humans by suctioning off their body salts—no fangs necessary.

A2. A.

A3. He decides they must be born pregnant.

A4. Because it has been poisoned by Arne Darvin, a Klingon in disguise, on Space Station K-7 where it was stored. The death of the tribbles revealed the problem.

A5. The sight of a Medusan can cause insanity in humanoids.

Q6. Who are Voles and where do they live?

    A. Voles are just like earth moles; they eat food on class-M planets.

    B. Voles are cyborg animals, designed by the Borgs as pets.

    C. Voles were left by the Cardassians on DS9, and live in the conduits.

    D. Voles are like tribbles, only not as cute. They cost half as much as tribbles, and can be bought at many space stations.

    E. Voles are pure energy creatures and invade the minds of Vulcans.

Q7. Name the 19th-century American who materializes on the *Enterprise* in "The Savage Curtain."

Q8. In "Evolution," we meet the Nanites. What are they?

Q9. Who—or what—was "Tin Man"?

    A. An Ozian android that has not emotion, but longs for it.

    B. A gigantic mechanical life-form that has intelligence and can travel the galaxy.

    C. A small metal ornament in the shape of a human, sought by the Ferengi for its monetary worth, much like the ancient "Maltese Falcon" of Earth legend.

    D. A derogatory name for Data.

Q10. The two-dimensional life-forms discovered in "The Loss," not only created a warp-drive malfunction, but had a serious effect on a crew member. Who was affected?

Q11. In "Galaxy's Child," actions of the *Enterprise* unintentionally resulted in maternal death. What mother dies in childbirth, and what becomes of her infant?

Q12. What attached itself like barnacles to the *Enterprise* in "Cost of Living"?

Q13. In "Quality of Life," what did the scientist Dr. Farallon invent that Data concluded was a life-form?

A6. C. Voles eat power cables, which is not so good on space stations.

A7. Abraham Lincoln.

A8. An intelligent species that evolved accidentally from robots used in medical situations.

A9. B is the correct answer for the creature in the episode of the same name—although D is also correct, as in "Skin of Evil." The tarry slime-monster Armus uses the term in the vain attempt to hurt Data's feelings.

A10. Deanna Troi suffered a temporary loss of her empathetic abilities.

A11. A gigantic space-living creature is the unfortunate mother. After she dies, her baby becomes "bonded" to the *Enterprise* and "nurses" from it, drawing power from its engines and nearly destroying the ship. The *Enterprise*, however, manages to wean the baby and point it in the direction of a group of its own kind, who will adopt it.

A12. A nonsentient life-form that had been living on an asteroid, destroyed by the *Enterprise* to prevent it from crashing into the planet Tessen III.

A13. Exocomp, a computerized brain capable of learning.

20

★★★★★
WHO'S WHO

QI. What other science-fiction television show did the actress who played Ensign Jenna D'Sora appear in?

Q2. What role did actor Sean Kenney play in "The Menagerie," and why?

Q3. One of the many objections NBC had to the first *Star Trek* pilot, "The Cage," was the role played by Majel Barrett, the future Mrs. Gene Roddenberry. What was the problem?

Q4. What was the full name of Khan, the charismatic figure found in suspended animation on the sleeper ship launched from Earth 200 years earlier?

Q5. In which episode of *Star Trek: The Next Generation* did Chakotay from *Voyager* appear?

Q6. What happened to Ensign Melora Pazlar in DS9?

Q7. Match the actors and the characters they played on *Deep Space Nine*:

1. Avery Brooks	A. Quark
2. Cirroc Lofton	B. Jake Sisko
3. Nana Visitor	C. Major Kira Nerys
4. Rene Auberjonis	D. Constable Odo
5. Terry Farrel	E. Lt. Jadzia Dax
6. Armin Shimerman	F. Cmdr. Benjamin Sisko
7. Siddig El Fadil	G. Chief Miles O'Brien
8. Colm Meany	H. Dr. Julian Bashir

A1. Michelle Scarabelli appeared as a regular cast member in *Alien Nation*.

A2. He played Captain Pike. The original Captain Pike, from the first pilot for *Star Trek* was played by Jeffrey Hunter. Considerable footage from that pilot, "The Cage" was reused, but a substitute had to be found for Hunter, who had declined to participate in the second pilot or in any reshooting for "The Menagerie." Since the Pike we now see is in a wheelchair and heavily bandaged, the substitution was easy, but in fact Sean Kenney looked a lot like Hunter, as can be seen in "Arena," in which he appeared as the navigator.

A3. She played Captain Pike's second-in-command, and the NBC brass didn't think audiences were ready for a woman to be shown in such a powerful position. The fact that she exuded more authority than anyone else, including a still very uncertain Leonard Nimoy, didn't help.

A4. Khan Noonien Singh, regarded as the foremost leader of the artificially bred men of the late 1990s. From 1992 to 1996, he had ruled a quarter of the Earth, from South Asia to the Middle East.

A5. "Journey's End"

A6. First, she was dropped from the series, though she was billed as being a permanent cast member. The reason she was dropped was because her character, who lived in a floating wheelchair, was too expensive.

A7. 1.–F., 2.–B., 3.–C., 4.–D., 5.–E., 6.–A., 7.–H., 8.–G.

Q8. If you watch the bar scenes closely on DS9, you'll notice an alien with a sad face in the background. Who is this?

Q9. Tim Russ, who plays Tuvok, the Vulcan security officer on *Voyager* has also had roles on other *Star Trek* series. He played T'Kar, a Klingon mercenary, in several episodes of DS9 and a humanoid terrorist in *Next Generation.* Who did he portray in the movie "*Generations*"?

Q10. The answer is "Genevieve Bujold." What is the question?

Q11. Crewman Mr. Kelowitz appeared in "Arena," "The *Galileo* Seven," and "This Side of Paradise." Name the actor who played him and the classic 1957 science-fiction movie in which he had the title role.

Q12. In "Operation—Annihilate!" William Shatner played two characters. Who was the second one?

Q13. What are SC937-0176CEC and S179-276SP?

Q14. Many feel that one of the finest guest star performances in *Star Trek* was the portrayal of Captain Mathew Decker in "The Doomsday Machine." Can you name the actor?

Q15. William Campbell, who played Trelane in "The Squire of Gothos," returned as a very different character in the second season. Name the character and the episode he appeared in.

Q16. If you were watching the HBO series, *Red Shoes Diary,* and saw a former *Star Trek* crew member semi-naked, who would that be:
A. Worf
B. Deanna Troi
C. James T. Kirk
D. Tasha Yar
E. All of the above—together.

Q17. Why does Ensign Garrovick play a key role in "Obsession"?

A8. Morn. Morn is an anagram for "Norm," a similar earthling character in another Paramount series, *Cheers.*

A9. A Starfleet tactical officer.

A10. Who was originally going to play the Captain on the *Voyager* series?

A11. Grant Woods of *The Incredible Shrinking Man.*

A12. The dead body of his elder brother George Samuel Kirk, who is a victim of the bat-like creatures (they also looked like very overdone omelets) that have invaded the planet Deneva.

A13. The Federation serial numbers of Captain Kirk and Spock, respectively.

A14. William Windom, best known in recent years as Seth, the Cabot Cove doctor on *Murder, She Wrote.*

A15. He returned as the Klingon Captain Koloth in "The Trouble with Tribbles."

A16. D, played by Denise Crosby.

A17. His father had been the captain of the U.S.S. *Farragut*, who had been killed by the vampire-cloud eleven years earlier while Kirk was serving a lieutenant on the ship.

Q18. Match the character on the left with the body that character borrowed:

1. Sargon   A. Dr. Ann Mulhall
2. Henoch   B. Spock
3. Thalassia   C. Kirk
                       D. Dr. Kate Pulaski
                       E. Miranda
                       F. Rosalind Shays

Q19. The characters of Gary Seven and Roberta Lincoln were left in place with futures open at the end of the episode "Assignment: Earth." What became of them?

Q20. A suggestion of the range of Gary Seven's powers was suggested by the fact that he was immune to what form of control?

Q21. One of Hollywood's most endearing "flakes," who would later co-star in *Close Encounters of the Third Kind,* made a vibrantly ditsy impression in "Assignment: Earth." Name her.

Q22. Who played the Gorgon?
A. F. Lee Bailey
B. Alan Derskowitz
C. Robert Shapiro
D. Melvin Belli
E. Joel Hyatt

Q23. The aliens are studying an empathic woman's reactions to human pain in "The Empath." What's the woman's name?

Q24. The highly sympathetic role of the dwarf jester, Alexander, on "Plato's Stepchildren," was nominated for Best Supporting Actor for the 1965 movie *Ship of Fools.* Name him.

Q25. Name the actress who played Losira.

Q26. What was the name of the first of Dr. Sevrin's followers to die on Eden?

A18. 1.–C. Sargon "borrowed" Kirk's body.
2.–B. Heroch "borrowed" Spock's body.
3.–A., D., E., and F. Thalassia took over the body of Diana Muldaur, who played Dr. Ann Mulhall (A) in "Return to Tomorrow." She went on to play Miranda (E) in "Is There In Truth No Beauty," Dr. Kate Puluski (D) in *Star Trek: The Next Generation*, and then Rosalind Shays (F) on *L.A. Law*.

A19. Nothing, ultimately. It was originally intended by the writers that they would continue in their own series but the concept did not sell, and no further episodes were filmed.

A20. A Vulcan nerve pinch.

A21. Teri Garr.

A22. A. F. Lee Bailey

A23. If you answered "Gem"—you're wrong. Dr. McCoy, not knowing her name, simply decided to call her "Gem." In fact, her name is never revealed.

A24. Michael Dunn, an actor of remarkable talents.

A25. Former Miss America Lee Meriwether.

A26. Adam.

Q27. Can you name the only actor to portray a Romulan, a Vulcan, and a Klingon?

Q28. In the opening episode of the new series, *Star Trek: The Next Generation*, "Encounter at Farpoint," several new crew members joined the *Enterprise*. Which of the following five was already aboard?

    A. William T. Riker
    B. Geordi La Forge
    C. Commander Data
    D. Dr. Beverly Crusher
    E. Wesley Crusher

Q29. How old was Wesley Crusher at this time?

Q30. Name the Starfleet admiral who traveled with Riker and the others on the U.S.S. *Hood* to the rendezvous with the *Enterprise* at Farpoint.

Q31. In "Haven" we are first introduced to a recurring character on *The Next Generation*. What *Enterprise* crew member is this person related to?

Q32. The answer to the immediately preceding question also was a regular, though secondary, character in the original *Star Trek* series, and had a voice-only role in *both* series. Who is it?

Q33. In "Where No One Has Gone Before," what is Starfleet propulsion expert Kosinski's odd assistant called?

Q34. Which late-20th-century American political figure is suggested by the actions of Admiral Mark Jameson when he was on the planet Mardan IV ("Too Short a Season")?

    A. Col. Oliver North
    B. Michael Huffington
    C. Newt Gingrich
    D. Rush Limbaugh

Q35. In "Datalore," the character of Lore, Data's older brother is first introduced. Data's family also included a father and a daughter. Who was the father and what actor played him? What was his daughter's name?

A27. Mark Lenard, who first appeared as the Romulan commander in "Balance of Terror," subsequently portrayed Spock's father Sarek, and appeared as a Klingon in *Star Trek: The Motion Picture.*

A28. C.

A29. He was fifteen.

A30. The aged Admiral Leonard McCoy.

A31. Lwaxana Troi is Deanna Troi's mother.

A32. Majel Barrett (Nurse Chapel in the original series and the voice of the ship's computer in both series), who also had a personal connection to the series—as Mrs. Gene Roddenberry.

A33. The Traveler.

A34. A. Col. Oliver North, who like Admiral Jameson, traded arms for hostages.

A35. Noonian Soong was his father (played under heavy aging makeup by Brent Spiner). Lal—Hindi for "beloved"—was his short-lived daughter.

Q36. Is it true or false that the family of Claire Raymond, as seen on Troi's desk-top viewer, contained the names of characters from *The Muppet Show* and *Gilligan's Island*?

Q37. The new season brought a new physician to the *Enterprise* to replace Dr. Crusher. What was the name of this character played by Diana Muldaur?

Q38. In anther television series, *L.A. Law*, how did Diana Muldaur's character die?

Q39. What does Commander Riker do for the second time in "The Icarus Factor"?

Q40. The offer of the new command is conveyed to Riker by his father, from whom he has long been estranged. What is his father's name?

Q41. In what region of Earth did Riker grow up?

Q42. What major change in the *Enterprise* crew roster was revealed at the start of the third season of *The Next Generation*?

Q43. To what rank have Geordi La Forge and Worf been promoted?

Q44. Who is Jeremy Aster, and what tragedy befalls him in "The Bonding"

Q45. Name the major *Enterprise* crew member who was born in Copernicus City, Luna in the year 2324.

Q46. In "Deja Q," what actor ends up at the end playing another member of the Q Continuum?

A36. It is true, although were not intended to be legible to the viewer.

A37. Dr. Katherine ("Kate") Pulaski.

A38. She fell down an elevator shaft.

A39. Declines a promotion to the rank of captain, to command the *Aires*, a scout ship.

A40. Kyle, who is a Starfleet civilian advisor.

A41. Alaska.

A42. After a year at Starfleet Medical, Dr. Beverly Crusher returns to her post while Kate Pulaski moves on.

A43. LaForge is now a lieutenant commander and Worf is a full lieutenant, and head of Security.

A44. His archeologist mother is killed by a mine remaining from an ancient war; the twelve-year-old boy had already lost his father.

A45. Dr. Beverly Crusher, daughter of Paul and Isabel Howard.

A46. Corbin Bernsen, better known as Arnie Becker, the divorce lawyer on *L.A. Law*.

Q47. Match the crewmember on the right with the experience on the left.

1. Miles O'Brien

A. Created holodeck images of Captain Picard and other bridge officers conforming to the programmer's fantasies.

2. Ensign Ro

B. Character's brain was taken over by aliens and enhanced to become a super-intelligent being.

3. Beverly Crusher

C. Had a fear of the transporter, which turned out to be justified by the presence of quasi-energy microbes in the transporter that were distorting the energy field.

4. Wesley Crusher

D. Helped Worf's son Alexander re-create the Old West in the holodeck.

5. Reginald Barclay

E. Helped solve the problem of what to do with Professor Moriarty who held the ship hostage until his desire to assume corporeal form was met.

Q48. Two seeming "ghosts" play a major part in "Brothers." Who are they?

Q49. In "Future Imperfect," despite being detained by an alien named Barash, Riker celebrates a birthday. How old is he?

Q50. Data assumes a "fatherly" role in two different ways on the episode "Data's Day." What are they?

A47. A.–5., B.–5., C.–5., D.–5., E.–5. Barclay was the character who had all of the experiences described.

A48. Data's creator, Dr. Noonien Soong, long believed dead, and Data's android brother Lore, supposedly destroyed near Omicron Theta in "Datalore."

A49. Thirty-two.

A50. He acts as father of the bride to Keiko Ishikawa at her marriage to Miles O'Brien in the Ten Forward Lounge, and we discover that he now has a pet cat, which it is subsequently revealed, he has named Spot in one of his charming confusions about human customs.

Q51. Family is a frequent theme in *The Next Generation*. Worf has adoptive parents, a son, and a biological brother, as well as an adoptive one. Picard has a brother and a nephew. In other episodes, Riker sees his father, Geordi misses him mom, Deanna is vexed by her meddlesome mother, and so on. In "Legacy," a former crewmember's relative shows up to cause trouble. Whose relative is it this time?

Q52. Before her special mission aboard the *Enterprise*, what had been the position of the Bajoran Ensign Ro Laren, as revealed in the episode named for her?

Q53. In "Hero Worship," who does the boy Timothy, rescued from the damaged research vessel *Vico*, begin to mimic on the *Enterprise*?

Q54. Who is Mr. Mot and what advice does he give Worf in "Schisms"?

Q55. Name the captain put in charge of the *Enterprise* in "Chain of Command" when Picard, Worf, and Beverly Crusher were sent on a secret mission into what turned out to be a Cardassian trap.

Q56. What musical composition is played by Neela, Data, and Ensign Cheney at a shipboard concert?

    A. Chopin's "Trio in G minor"
    B. "Heart and Soul"
    C. "Chopsticks"
    D. Chopin's "Minuet Waltz"
    E. Beethoven's "Ode to Joy"

Q57. To what ship was Lieutenant Riker posted at the end of "Second Chances"?

Q58. What was the name of Commander Sisko's wife?

    A. Jen
    B. Jennifer
    C. Jenny
    D. Jen Jen
    E. Jen-fer

A51. The sister of the late Tasha Yar, Ishara Yar. Some of Tasha's other relations mean trouble, too: her daughter (of rape by Romulan officer) shows up many episodes later to plot against the Federation on behalf of the Romulan Empire and some Klingon renegades.

A52. She had been imprisoned for terrorism, for an attack at Solarian IV that turns out to have been staged by the Cardassians.

A53. Data—a sensible choice for a child traumatized by shock.

A54. He is the *Enterprise* barber, and he suggests that Worf start using a conditioner because of all the wind and dry air Worf encounters on Away missions.

A55. Captain Edward Jellico.

A56. A.

A57. The U.S.S. *Gandhi*, leaving open the possibility of a further storyline.

A58. B.

Q59. In "The Outrageous Okona," Okona spends much of his time trying to seduce female *Enterprise* crewmembers, including a transporter officer played by an actress who later went on to star in her own series. Who was the actress?

Q60. How did Sisko's wife die?

Q61. What was the name of the Cardassian who was Oto's former boss on DS9?

Q62. In the DS9 episode, "The Homecoming" what was the name of the Bajoran war hero whom Quark discovered was still alive?

Q63. Who were Ruth Bonaventure, Magda Kovacs, and Eve McHuron?

Q64. The brides were intended for the settlers on Ophiucus III. Did triple wedding bills ring, or not?

Q65. In "The Realm of Fear," Geordi says, "Transporting really is the safest way to travel." To whom is he talking?

A59. Teri Hatcher of *Lois and Clark*.

A60. She died in the battle against the Borg at Wolf 359.

A61. Gul Dukat.

A62. Li Nalas.

A63. Harry Mudd's mail order brides on "Mudd's Women."

A64. They did, but not for the settlers. The lithium miners on Rigel XIII ended up as the lucky grooms.

A65. Poor Lt. Reginald Barclay, who has developed "fear of transporting."

★★★★★
EXTRA CREDIT

In which show episode or movie did the these ships first appear?

Q1. Adelphi	**Q19.** Charleston
Q2. Agamemnon	**Q20.** Cochrane
Q3. Ahwahnne	**Q21.** Constantinople
Q4. Ajax	**Q22.** Constellation
Q5. Akagi	**Q23.** Constellation
Q6. Antares	**Q24.** Constitution
Q7. Archon	**Q25.** Copernicus
Q8. Arcos	**Q26.** Crazy Horse
Q9. Aries	**Q27.** Defiant
Q10. Bellerephon	**Q28.** Denver
Q11. Berlin	**Q29.** Drake
Q12. Biko	**Q30.** Eagle
Q13. Bozeman	**Q31.** Endeavor
Q14. Bradbury	**Q32.** Enterprise C
Q15. Brattain	**Q33.** Essex
Q16. Buran	**Q34.** Excalibur
Q17. Cairo	**Q35.** Excelsior
Q18. Carolina	**Q36.** Exeter

A1. "Tin Man" (TNG)

A2. "Descent" (TNG)

A3. "Best of Both Worlds" (TNG)

A4. "Tapestry" (TNG)

A5. "Redemption" (TNG)

A6. "Charlie X" (TREK)

A7. "Return of the Archons" (TREK)

A8. "Legacy" (TNG)

A9. "The Icarus Factor" (TNG)

A10. "Redemption" (TNG)

A11. "Angel One" (TNG)

A12. "Fistfull of Datas" (TNG)

A13. "Cause and Effect" (TNG)

A14. "Menage a Troi" (TNG)

A15. "Night Terrors" (TNG)

A16. "The Best of Both Worlds" (TNG)

A17. "Chain of Command" (TNG)

A18. "Friday's Child" (TREK)

A19. "The Neutral Zone" (TNG)

A20. "Emissary" (DS9)

A21. "The Schizoid Man" (TNG)

A22. "The Doomsday Machine" (TREK)

A23. "The Battle" (TNG)

A24. "Space Seed" (TNG)

A25. TREK Movies

A26. "Descent" (TNG)

A27. "The Tholian Web" (TREK) / Deep Space Nine

A28. "Ethics" (TNG)

A29. "The Arsenal of Freedom" (TNG)

A30. TREK Movies

A31. "Redemption" (TNG)

A32. "Yesterday's Enterprise" (TNG)

A33. "Power Play" (TNG)

A34. "The Ultimate Computer" (TREK) "Redemption" (TNG)

A35. TREK Movies 3 and 6

A36. "The Omega Glory" (TREK)

Q37. *Farragut*

Q38. *Fearless*

Q39. *Firebrand*

Q40. *Gage*

Q41. *Gandhi*

Q42. *Ganges*

Q43. *Gettysberg*

Q44. *Goddard*

Q45. *Gorkon*

Q46. *Grissom*

Q47. *Hathaway*

Q48. *Hermes*

Q49. *Hood*

Q50. *Horatio*

Q51. *Horizon*

Q52. *Hornet*

Q53. *Intrepid*

Q54. *Jenolen*

Q55. *Kyushu*

Q56. *Lalo*

Q57. *Lantree*

Q58. *LaSalle*

Q59. *Lexington*

Q60. *Magellan*

Q61. *Mekong*

Q62. *Melbourne*

Q63. *Merrimac*

Q64. *Monitor*

Q65. *Odyssey*

Q66. *Orinoco*

Q67. *Pasteur*

Q68. *Pegasus*

Q69. *Phoenix*

Q70. *Potemkin*

Q71. *Princeton*

Q72. *Prometheus*

Q73. *Reliant*

Q74. *Renegade*

Q75. *Republic*

Q76. *Repulse*

A37. (TREK)

A38. "Where No One Has Gone Before" (*TNG*)

A39. "The Best of Both Worlds" (*TNG*)

A40. "Emissary" (*TNG*)

A41. "Second Chances" (*TNG*)

A42. *Deep Space Nine*

A43. "Too Short A Season" (*TNG*)

A44. "The Vengeance Factor" (*TNG*)

A45. "Descent" (*TNG*)

A46. (TREK) movie #3 and "The Most Toys" (*TNG*)

A47. "Peak Performance" (*TNG*)

A48. "Redemption" (*TNG*)

A49. "The Ultimate Computer" (*TREK*) / "Tin Man" (*TNG*)

A50. "Conspiracy" (*TNG*)

A51. "Piece of the Action" (*TREK*)

A52. "Redemption" (*TNG*)

A53. "Court Martial" (*TREK*) / "Family" (*TNG*)

A54. "Relics" (*TNG*)

A55. "The Best of Both Worlds" (*TNG*)

A56. "We'll Always Have Paris" (*TNG*)

A57. "Unnatural Selection" (*TNG*)

A58. "Reunion" (*TNG*)

A59. "The Ultimate Computer" (*TREK*)

A60. "Starship Mine" (*TNG*)

A61. *Deep Space Nine*

A62. "The Best of Both Worlds" (*TNG*)

A63. "Sarek" (*TNG*)

A64. "The Defector" (*TNG*)

A65. "Dominion" (*DS9*)

A66. *Deep Space Nine*

A67. "All Good Things" (*TNG*)

A68. "The Pegasus" (*TNG*)

A69. "The Wounded" (*TNG*)

A70. "Turnabout Intruder" (*TREK*) / "Legacy" (*TNG*)

A71. "The Best of Both Worlds" (*TNG*)

A72. "Second Sight" (*DS9*)

A73. TREK Movies

A74. "Conspiracy" (*TNG*)

A75. "Court Martial" (*TREK*)

A76. "The Child" (*TNG*)

Q77. *Rio Grande*

Q78. *Rutledge*

Q79. *Saratoga*

Q80. *Stargazer*

Q81. *Sutherland*

Q82. *Thomas Paine*

Q83. *Tian Nan Men*

Q84. *Tolstoy*

Q85. *Trieste*

Q86. *Tripoli*

Q87. *Tsiolkovsky*

Q88. *Valiant*

Q89. *Vico*

Q90. *Victory*

Q91. *Wellington*

Q92. *Yamato*

Q93. *Yangtzee Kiang*

Q94. *Yorktown*

Q95. *Yosemite*

Q96. *Zapata*

Q97. *Zhukov*

A77. *Deep Space Nine*

A78. "The Wounded" (*TNG*)

A79. TREK Movie 4 / "The Emissary" (*DS9*)

A80. "The Battle" (*TNG*)

A81. "Redemption" (*TNG*)

A82. "Conspiracy" (*TNG*)

A83. "Redemption" (*TNG*)

A84. "The Best of Both Worlds" (*TNG*)

A85. "Clues" (*TNG*)

A86. "Datalore" (*TNG*)

A87 "The Naked Now" (*TNG*)

A88. "A Taste of Armageddon" (*TREK*)

A89. "Hero Warship" (*TNG*)

A90. "Identity Crisis" (*TNG*)

A91. "Ensign Ro" (*TNG*)

A92. "Contagion" (*TNG*)

A93. *Deep Space Nine*

A94. "Obsession" (*TREK*)

A95. "Realm of Fear" (*TNG*)

A96. "Menage a Troi" (*TNG*)

A97. "Hollow Pursuits" (*TNG*)

About the Author

Peggy Robin is the vice-president of Adler & Robin Books, Inc., a literary agency. She is the author of numerous books including *Saving the Neighborhood: You Can Fight Developers and Win!* (Woodbine House), *Outwitting Toddlers* (Lowell House), *How to Be a Successful Fertility Patient* (William Morrow & Company), *Bottlefeeding Without Guilt: A Reassuring Guide for Loving Parents* (Prima Publishing), and *The Starfleet Academy Entrance Exam* (Birch Lane Press).

Her books have received wide acclaim. *Saving the Neighborhood* was featured with a full-page entry in the millenium edition of *The Whole Earth Catalog*.

Here are some reviews of Peggy Robin's Books:

Saving the Neighborhood

Seldom does one encounter a book with such a wealth of useful information about neighborhood preservation...An excellent field manual for both the veteran and novice community activist.—*The Neighborhood Works*

This just might be the best $16.95 investment you can make...For people who understand that the integrity of their neighborhoods, communities, natural surroundings and ways of life are of the utmost importance.—*Small Town Magazine*

Attractively designed, well-written, thoughtful, comprehensive, and to the point.—*Planning Magazine*

A pragmatic activist handbook...demystifies the planning and zoning process and provides practical advice on forming a community organization...gives useful 'nitty-gritty' advice.—*Library Journal*

Old hands will find this book a good reference, and beginners can use it to learn the process, from talking to politicians to preservation ordinances, to what to do after you win...Robin maintains it's a war...Her book helps with strategy.—*Booklist*

How to Be a Successful Ferility Patient

Important and supportive information to help infertile couples through the fertility treatment process... an excellent work.—Sharon N. Covington, Director of Counseling, The Shady Grove Fertility Center.

The extensive interviews with dozens of male and female infertility patients in this helpful book represent virtually every etiology of infertility and appropriate means of treatment available today...Accurate and realistic.—*Fertility News*

Excellent...chock full of information that I haven't seen elsewhere.—Susan Cooper, author of *The Long-Awaited Stork*

Peggy Robin lives in Washington, D.C., with her husband, Bill, and two children, Karen and Claire.